Just Five Days Till Friday

Just Five Days Till Friday

LELA GILBERT

ACCENT BOOKS
Denver, Colorado

MEMBER OF
EVANGELICAL CHRISTIAN
PUBLISHERS ASSOCIATION

Third Printing, 1980

ACCENT BOOKS
A division of Accent-B/P Publications, Inc.
12100 W. Sixth Avenue
P.O. Box 15337
Denver, Colorado 80215

Library of Congress Catalog Card Number: 78-74204

ISBN 0-89636-022-9

I needn't spend my lifetime
Forgotten on God's shelf.
He uses broken vessels.
He fills them with Himself.

To Mother and Daddy, who prayed.
To Glen, who picked up the pieces.

Contents

Before We Begin . . .

It was a hot, late-summer day in downtown Los Angeles. I was eighteen—an immature eighteen at that—and I had just been hired for my very first job. I was to be a clerk at a large department store.

Far from feeling joyful, I was instead filled with dread and alarm. As an only child, my parents had always provided for me. I had a long history of bad health and, as I made the gigantic step into the world of employment, I was tormented by the fear of failure.

When I expressed my feelings to my friend Phil, I expected a kind outpouring of sympathy and pity. Instead, with mild irritation he looked me in the eye and said, "Oh, come on! Be a citizen of the world. Everybody works!"

Of course I resented his uncompassionate reaction, but deep inside I realized he was right. And I hoped, somehow, that God could help me meet the challenge, since I was a Christian.

Well . . . it took a lot of years and a lot of unpleasant experiences for me to become a "citizen of the world."

Working has never been easy for me—emotional, moody and undisciplined person that I am. But one thing has made itself clear. The deeper my relationship with God has grown, the better employee I have become. God's love, God's wisdom, God's Spirit have all worked through me, making me more kind, more responsible, more approachable and more valuable to my employer.

Because my Christian life has played such a major part in my career, this book is more specifically about Christian commitment than simply about working.

Humanly speaking, I don't have any more answers to life's problems than the next person. If a person who will not accept God's answers to life's hardships comes to me with a problem, I usually find myself stammering around: The only answers I know are the answers God gives to His children; the only solutions I have are the ones He has given to me time and time again when I had no one to turn to but Him.

So, I'll have to ask you before we even begin to look at work together: *Have you met Jesus Christ?* Do you believe He is God's Son? That He loves you? That He died for you and now lives? Have you given Him your future? Doing that is much more important than any other thing I could say to you. Give God your life, your future. It is the greatest opportunity for success, financial security, joy and peace of mind that exists in our world.

But maybe you already are a committed Christian. And maybe you're a woman like me—you have to go to work tomorrow! If so, this book was written especially for you. Because, unless you love your job more than life itself, you occasionally awaken with a jolt on Monday morning, dreading the week ahead.

And perhaps you, like me, have whispered to yourself as you gazed grimly into the early morning looking-glass, "Cheer up, friend. *Just Five Days Till Friday!*"

1
Monday
What Am I Doing Here?

The porcelain alarm screamed its shrill message into the cool, dark morning. Carolyn awoke, lay beneath the warm, comforting blankets for a few last drowsy minutes, sighed and crawled out of bed.

After plugging in the percolator, she turned up the heater and stood in front of it as the fragrance of brewing coffee began to fill the house. The world outside the windows looked like a portrait in black and white, with one apricot cloud blushing across the mountains where the sun would soon appear.

"What a beautiful morning," she thought. "I could sit for hours and watch the colors change. And how I would love to walk awhile, breathing the crystal air."

She poured her coffee, sat down, then realized she had better be thinking more realistic thoughts like, "What time is it? What shall I wear today? Will the car start?"

When she was dressed and in some semblance of order, Carolyn jumped into her old VW, which mercifully started, and drove a bit too fast toward work. She raced through the office door four minutes late (no one would notice), and immediately began to feel a familiar, trapped sensation. *Where has the beautiful morning gone? Whose are all these sullen Monday faces? What am I doing here?*

What am I doing here? How many times at how many jobs have I asked myself that very question?

Why do women work? Usually it's a necessity of life. If you are single and haven't been blessed with a large inheritance or a benevolent aunt, chances are you have a job. If you are married but want to build a better financial foundation for yourself and your husband, you probably work. It's a good means of staying alive!

And, too, there are women, financially comfortable though they may be, who enjoy getting out of the house and keeping themselves busy. They like the contact with people, enjoy the feeling of accomplishment—and the extra money, too.

Then there are women who have deeper purposes, such as serving mankind or God, or proving to themselves that they are capable. They may work in public service, charity work or through religious organizations. Quite frequently, the amount of financial compensation they receive is not as great as what they might earn elsewhere.

With each reason for working comes a different set of attitudes . . . and problems.

"I'm here to make money" is probably the most common answer to the "Why do you work?" question. In today's economy, some women simply cannot quit working. Often, feelings of resentment arise from that situation. There is, from time to time, a sense of enclosure—*Help! I'm stuck!*

Dissatisfaction with her present position sometimes follows: *Surely I could be making more money than this—what cheapskates they are!* Many a woman scans the want ads day after day with a fresh supply of resumes in her drawer just waiting to be mailed off. Surely somewhere out there awaits The Perfect Job!

Along with a feeling of dissatisfaction, women who must work for survival may experience feelings of insecurity. Bosses come and go, new faces arrive on the scene, mistakes are made. And a strange foreboding begins to stir inside—*What if I lose my job?* Insomnia, fear and more resentment are by-products of this type of insecurity.

There is another all-too-familiar sensation—greed! *I'm going to make every dime I can!* Coffee breaks lengthen; there is a tendency to stretch out the work load so overtime will be necessary. Sometimes taking on a little more than can reasonably be handled is an effective means of bringing in those precious time-and-a-half dollars.

The woman who doesn't have to work as a means of survival is faced with few of these dilemmas, at least at first. In fact, she may not take her job too seriously. She'll do what she is given to do, probably very well, but that's all she cares to accomplish. But then, one day she takes her first few paychecks in hand and merrily goes shopping for herself. After that, the old money-making motivation just may take over after all!

There are entirely different frustrations for the woman who has a deeper purpose as her work-reason. She may feel held back by co-workers. She may find that others are not as dedicated as she is. She may experience a desire to accept more and more responsibility just to see that things are done right.

Failure can break her heart, and maybe even cause her to give up. Money is not the important thing. It is success—whatever that success means in her particular case. And she'll do her best to achieve it.

If you're a Christian woman who works, what should your motivation—your work-reason—be? Where does God fit into your attitudes? Your goals? Your frustrations?

Perhaps the answers to these questions can best be found by beginning at the beginning. Why did you take the job you now have? At the time, did you feel it was God's will? If you are *very* unhappy now, it may be that God doesn't really want you where you are, or your reason for being there is finished. These possibilities are some things you will need to examine in prayer.

But if any of you lacks wisdom, let him ask of God, who gives to all men generously and without reproach, and it will be given to him.

But let him ask in faith without any doubting, for the one who doubts is like the surf of the sea driven and tossed by the wind (James 1:5, 6).

Ask God for wisdom. But remember the poor double-minded man in the Book of James: Be sure you're expecting an answer, and are willing to accept whatever answer you receive.

In the absence of very strong positive feelings that God (and not just we ourselves) wants us to change jobs, it would be foolish to assume that whenever we feel dissatisfaction at work, we aren't where we belong. Such emotions come and go and shouldn't be allowed to control our lives. After all, there is *no* Perfect Job.

Some think that the ideal job for a Christian is in Christian service. Once I decided just that.

I had worked in the area of retail fashion for three or four years, but I began to think of it as an unworthy vocation. *Too shallow, too materialistic,* I judged. And I began to look for work in a more humanitarian vein.

My search led me to the psychiatric out-patient clinic of a large Los Angeles hospital. An ad was in the paper; 50 or more of us answered it. It sounded to me like a marvelous opportunity to do something for someone less fortunate. And after all, I'd had one whole semester of psychology.

After several interviews, the people in charge came up with three likely subjects—myself and two others. We would each have one more interview; after that, the decision would be made. Of course I expected to get the job. Had God not shown me that I should change fields? Do something worthwhile? Help my fellow man?

I really prayed before that last interview. I told the Lord that if this was what He wanted me to do, He would have to give me all the right answers. I prepared myself continuously for any "trick" psychological questions that might be thrown my way. (Don't make Freudian remarks . . . don't say you like your father better than your mother . . . don't be negative about disturbed individuals).

I arrived at the interview, prepared to the hilt. As I awaited my turn, praying all the while, I watched the psychiatric patients come and go as I sat in the waiting room thinking that very soon I would be helping them in some small way.

At last my name was called. The large, tough-looking woman who was to interview me had four people in her office when I entered. The phone was ringing frantically. She completed her dangling conversations, answered more calls and at last sighed and looked at me.

I cheerily remarked, "This is a real madhouse, isn't it?" She smiled tolerantly, and realizing my gross error, I quickly countered, "It's enough to drive you crazy!"

Needless to say, I didn't get that job. I was really surprised at God. Where had He been when I needed Him? Why in the world didn't He help me get a nice wholesome job like that? I prayed, *OK, Lord. If You want me to work, You're going to have to send the job to me. I'm not looking for any more worthy vocations!*

Two days later my phone rang. A friend for whom I had worked earlier in my career was calling, asking if I would come to work for her as Assistant Fashion/ Publicity Director at a lovely Westside department store. I concluded that this was where God wanted me. And it was!

God needs people *everywhere*. And in virtually every area of legitimate employment, God will place a strategic Christian to shine as a light. It's not up to us to decide what a worthy vocation is—it's up to Him. He doesn't care about fashion/publicity, finance, education, or whatever the field of secular endeavor, nearly so much as He cares that one of His children is communicating His love to a little group of people who cross his path.

While I was working as a copywriter for a department store (years after the previous incident) I overheard that the Display Department was looking for extra help. I really didn't have enough work to do in Advertising, and I felt certain that God was speaking to me, asking me to volunteer my services to Display, where I'd had earlier experience.

Sure enough, they accepted me with open arms— for two weeks. In that short period I had the opportunity to share God's love with two searching people. Then the Director politely told me that they had too many people in Display after all! You see— God used me for His purposes, then put me back where I began.

That's such a good thing to keep in mind as we work. It's not the job that's so important to God—it's our lives reflecting His life that He's concerned with. And although you can be sure that He'll help you with your problems on the job, you can be even more sure that He'll put you exactly where He wants *you* to shine.

With that thought, it isn't so hard to handle the frustrations of the circumstances we're in.

One occupational hazard that exists in any kind of employment—whether you like what you do or not, and whether you want to work or have to—is putting a job too high on the priority list. And don't be fooled! It can happen to any of us.

Sometimes insecurity does it—makes us try too hard. Sometimes it is dedication, sometimes it's devotion to a boss, or just a determination to succeed. But one thing is certain: When we put a job ahead of God, ahead of others, sometimes even ahead of our own personal lives, we do not find fulfillment.

I once knew a man who received a beautiful opportunity from the Lord. It came in the form of a job that he had dreamed of all his life. And he was delighted.

He gave God due credit and thanked Him. He told his wife that he would now be able to provide for her in a far better way. And he was thrilled that at last his parents would be really proud of him.

The man began to work, then began to work longer and longer hours. Sometimes at home he could only find time to read the paper and sleep. Sometimes he didn't even go home.

He lost touch with parents and friends because he was too wrapped up in his job to communicate with them about anything else. He lost touch with his wife because he was too tired to talk to her at all. He eventually found himself with no wife, few friends, and out of fellowship with God. And he very nearly lost the job, too.

Dedication? Yes, he had that. But insecurity and determination were also factors in his "success." This man's story is not an isolated incident. It happens *every* day—to men *and* to women.

Another course that job priority problems can take is of a more negative nature. A young woman whom I greatly admire for her deep Christian love holds a somewhat unrewarding secretarial position. When she and I converse, quite often her job is all she can find to talk about. She doesn't realize how much of her energy is expended in reliving unpleasant circumstances, in sorting out people's motives and attitudes. This woman doesn't really like her job at all; she just can't put it out of her mind.

There is an old Sunday school jingle that spells out the secret of genuine joy:

> J-esus First
> O-thers Second
> Y-ourself Last

Maybe it is simplistic, but if you think about it, *first* the Lord gave you your job. *Second,* the other people you work with are the reason you are there. And *last* comes you—your success, your money, your needs. And these are side-effects, not purposes.

God is really our employer. He has put our bosses

over us to direct us. We are accountable to them; when we work, our time is their time. We must always be responsible and dependable, while keeping our priorities in focus.

> Whatever you do, do your work heartily, as for the Lord rather than for men; knowing that from the Lord you will receive the reward of the inheritance. It is the Lord Christ whom you serve (Colossians 3:23, 24).

If you don't have to work but do so to keep busy, God is *your* boss, too! When you concentrate on His approval, you will find that laziness and inaccuracy seldom find their way into your style.

If you are working for a purpose or goal other than money, you may find that from time to time your idealism dulls a bit. You may become frustrated by the seeming callousness of those with whom you work. It is unbelievably easy to think that others are not as spiritual, as dedicated, as capable as we when we are trying our best to serve God. We should beware the habit of judging others.

You will probably find that your resentments rapidly diminish when you remind yourself that God has placed you in your circumstances so that you can be of service to Him. What an adventure it is! Who could feel trapped for long in the personal service of the King?

Those of you who are working mothers faced with the priority of a higher responsibility to your children can be sure that God, your *real* employer, understands your situation and your problems.

When your child is ill, when he has school problems or personal needs that must be dealt with, our Lord knows where you and your priorities must be—with your child.

God will look out for you and will make the way smooth for you if you ask Him. If you have an employer who is really unsympathetic to your child-related circumstances, it may be a good indication that you are not in the right job after all.

And my God shall supply all your needs according to His riches in glory in Christ Jesus (Philippians 4:19).

We have assurance, a *promise*, that our needs will be supplied. No Christian who believes these words should allow himself even a moment of worry about money. (That's not to say that we *won't*, but we *shouldn't*.)

Jesus said that He would provide for our needs. He said that our Father is concerned about the little sparrows and the lilies of the field—and how much more about us! And He said that we need only seek Him and His righteousness and all the rest would be added to us.

Are you a worrier? Do you worry about financial security, job security, *insecurity?* If we would take time to examine the work-related tension that we experience, we would find that a large part of it comes down to *What do they think of me?* Insecurity, like financial security, can be entrusted to God, if we are doing the best we can on our job. Our purpose in work, as in everything, is to glorify God. He will take care of everything else.

No matter why we work, where we work, when we work: If we are truly working as God's servants, we need to keep it well in mind that God has already accomplished His purpose. He has put you where you are, me where I am, and He has put all the others where they are, too. He is working in all our lives, loving us dearly, helping each of us to grow toward Him in a different way. He *will* be glorified. All we need to do is our best—the results are His, because success always has been and always will be His responsibility, anyway!

> But thanks be to God, who gives us the victory through our Lord Jesus Christ. Therefore, my beloved brethren, be steadfast, immovable, always abounding in the work of the Lord, knowing that your toil is not in vain in the Lord (I Corinthians 15:57, 58).

Well . . .
Here I am at work again, Lord.
But I know that You've put me where I am, so I'll stay.
And when You move me on, I'll be glad to go.
I'll do my best for You while I do my work,
And when I speak and act, I'll try to share Your
love with as many as will listen and see.

I'll put You first, all the others second,
And me last.
And let the glory be Yours, Lord.
(Oh . . . by the way, thanks for the job!)

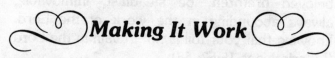 **Making It Work**

1. List as many reasons as you can for being thankful
   to God for the job that you have. (Then thank Him!)
2. Write down the problems and frustrations that you face
   at your job. After listing each difficulty, think about
   what you can do as a Christian to solve it. Ask God to help
   you.
3. Set goals for yourself of ways that you can be a better
   "Light" at your job. Check your list periodically to see
   how you're growing.

2
Tuesday
What's My Problem?

Kate loved her job at the department store. It was interesting, different from anything she had done before. Today she was especially excited because she was to be a dresser for a large fashion show which would take place in the late afternoon. She had only seen two or three fashion shows before and certainly had never been backstage.

She was curious. What would the models be like? Would they be snooty and sophisticated? Would they be impressed by the beautiful clothes, as she would?

When the time arrived, she rushed to the store restaurant, found the dressing room and took a quick look around her. Some of the models had arrived with their big, expensive tote bags, their rollered hair wrapped in designer scarves. A few sat about, wearing little but their pantyhose, talking and smoking. They seemed relaxed and unaware of the aura of glamour that filled the room.

It wasn't that they were so pretty—some weren't really pretty at all. They were just incredibly perfect-looking, from the way their make-up was applied to the smoothness of their skin and the slimness of their bodies.

As Kate stood quietly waiting for someone to notice her, she suddenly felt as if she had shrunk three or four inches. And gained twenty or thirty pounds. She became increasingly aware of the chipped places in her nail polish; the run in her nylons that she thought no one would notice; the brand new blemishes that had appeared unannounced that morning. She felt *plain*. And unfeminine. All at once she wanted to run out of the room, to disappear.

Trying to pull herself together she thought, *What's happening to my self-esteem? Why do I feel so small and insignificant? What's my problem?*

Is it really so unusual to feel insecure and self-conscious? Not at all. All of us at one time or another have had days when we felt ugly and blotchy, generally unattractive.

But some of us feel that way more than once in awhile. It gets to be a habit to apologize for our looks, to joke about our weight, to make excuses for the things we don't like about ourselves. We find it hard to walk through a room without feeling foolish, and notice that depression is a common occurrence in our private lives.

Of course, personal appearance isn't and shouldn't

be the most important thing in anyone's life. But we live in a very visual world, and the way we look often affects the way we are treated and the way we treat others. Even personality isn't as important, at least as a first impression, as the way we look. Try as we might to philosophize away physical appearance, it is a very big item in today's world.

I feel that I have looked on this matter of physical appearance from both sides. I have been both bad-looking and good-looking. When I was a six-weeks-old baby, I broke out in what appeared to be an infant eczema, sure to clear up in a week or two. I was twenty-one when it finally went away!

For all those years I was virtually disfigured by a *most* unsightly skin condition—face, hands, feet, legs, just about everywhere on my body. Believe me, it took its toll in self-confidence. I was overweight, too, which didn't help matters at all. And when I was in high school, a teacher told me that I had the most negative personality he had ever encountered. I was a real winner! No wonder, at eighteen, I had never been out on a date.

After years of wondering why *I* had to be different, after much anger and bitterness toward God and toward people who "looked on the outward appearance," I snidely told the Lord that if He could do better with my life—go ahead and try.

The first thing He did was teach me to accept myself the way He had made me—broken out and not very attractive. *Then* He healed my skin. *Then* He put me in circumstances—my job—where I *had* to lose weight, to dress tastefully, to apply make-up well, to wear my hair in a current style.

Within six years, I was a fashion model at one of Los Angeles' most elegant department stores. Every day people told me I was beautiful. I was even asked how I managed to have such lovely clear skin! All I could ever answer was that God had made me over into a new person—from the *inside* to the *outside*, beyond what I could ask.

> Now to Him who is able to do exceeding abundantly beyond all that we ask or think, according to the power that works within us (Ephesians 3:20).

So, how about you? Are there physical problems relating to your personal appearance that you can't change? Have you given them to God? Can you honestly thank Him for them? Good. Now—on to the things you *can* change!

Weight seems to be the biggest hang-up with women today. A few women are underweight and have to work at staying over 100 pounds. But for most of us the battle is far different. Large size clothing is becoming big business (pardon the expression) and in the United States, health clubs and spas are incredibly profitable.

Studies have shown that most women are at least ten pounds overweight. So what about it? Does it matter?

Do you not know that you are a temple of God,
and that the Spirit of God dwells in you?
(I Corinthians 3:16).

You see, God cares about your weight problem! He
is concerned about the way you look. It's true—I
know. And prayer is a real help when you've got weight
to lose. Ask God to remind you of your goal and to give
you strength. And then remember, the mental formula
for losing weight is as simple as this: *Which is more
important, what I'm about to eat or the way I want to
look a few months from now?* If the food is more
important, you'll stay overweight. If you *really* want to
lose the weight, you will.

Make up your mind about it: See your doctor, then
think "thin" when you are about to eat. Start counting
calories. It's not a gimmick—3,500 calories equal 1
pound. If you are trying to lose a pound, eat 3,500
calories less than you need to burn. (If you want to gain
a pound, eat 3,500 more.) Depending on how much
you want to lose, a diet of between 1,000 and 1,500
calories a day should produce results.

Use your imagination. Find every interesting, tasty
way you can for preparing your daily calories. Watch
out for hidden calories in salad dressings, mayonnaise
and snack foods. Eat lots of protein. Vegetables are a
marvelous diet food because they are tasty and
contain few calories. Drinking a lot of liquids will help
keep you feeling less hungry. And allow a sweet treat
once in awhile to keep up your morale. You will be
amazed at the results!

People today are becoming more and more aware of nutrition—and well they should. They are learning that certain foods aren't good for them while others are vital. When you are dieting, good nutrition is a *must*. Your meals, no matter how small, should be well-balanced, containing all the necessary food groups.

My personal opinion, from study and observation, is that most fad or crash diets are a waste of time. Diets that limit you to *all* protein, *just* bananas or *all* the ice cream you can eat are cheating you out of a lot of important food properties.

Once you have your trim figure, you'll want to dress well. Looking nice in clothes has little to do with spending lots of money. It *does* have to do with careful choice of basic clothing, a sense of color and the clever use of accessories.

In dressing, forget the cliches you've heard. Wearing pink doesn't make you more feminine. Lavishing yourself in lace doesn't guarantee that you will look lady-like. Neither does tweed represent masculinity. It is the woman inside the clothes who makes the difference. So, the question is, what makes *you* feel attractive? Search to find the look that is "you" and stick with it.

If you're on a budget—and if you work I'm sure you are—buy skirts, trousers, blouses and jackets that interchange so you can stretch your wardrobe and not be bored with it. Dresses are great but lack versatility, so be selective.

Choose your colors carefully. Buy pieces of clothir in colors which coordinate or contrast with things yc already own. Avoid extreme fashion fads, which ter to be wasteful because they enter and exit the fashic scene so quickly.

Choose your fabrics carefully, too. Some of today new synthetics are amazingly easy to care for, but the don't have the good looks of naturals like cotton, wo and silk. Often a good compromise is a "blend" fabr which incorporates the attractiveness of the natura and the easy-care qualities and lower cost of tl synthetics.

Dressing stylishly on a budget invariably raises tl question, "How can I invest in clothing that won't : out of style in two or three years? What can I buy th won't look "out of it" next fall when I drag it out of t! back of my closet for an encore?"

"Classic" dressing is always in style. Lengths skirts or pants may vary somewhat, but changi hems is a lot easier than changing wardrobes. And, course, considerably less expensive.

What is classic dressing? Simple, tailored clothes traditional sportswear designers are the classics, t good investments year in and year out. For examp select two or three skirts that brush the leg from t bottom of the knee to just midcalf. If current style just below the knee when you purchase the skirt, sure that there is a reasonably wide hem 1 wearability in coming years. Stay away from very 1 or very narrow skirt silhouettes.

If you like to wear pants, again, choose seve

classic styles. A waistband with one or no pleats and a not-too-wide leg that just touches the top of the foot without "breaking" (bending) is a classic pants shape. Cuffs are a matter of personal taste. If the pants aren't too wide or too narrow, cuffs won't look dated.

Avoid heavily pleated trousers which go in and out of style with regularity. And bear in mind that giant bell-bottoms as well as super-tapered styles are not likely to be around forever.

Jackets should be chosen for their fit. Lapels should not be extremely narrow or extremely wide. Jacket length can vary, but short jackets tend to be of a more right-today, wrong-tomorrow nature.

Sweaters are generally good investments, and shirt and blouse styles don't change a great deal from year to year.

Style—as well as color and fabric choice—can disguise many a figure flaw. Tunics, for example, can hide wide hips; pants can cover not-so-pretty knees. On the contrary, too-tight pants will make you look heavier than you really are, as will a bra that doesn't support you properly.

Accessories also can disguise figure flaws, by drawing attention away from the area. Collect scarves; they are so versatile. There are dozens of ways scarves can be tied creatively to change and enhance the appearance of a basic wardrobe. Here's your chance to show some ingenuity.

Stylish shoes, bags, and jewelry are relatively inexpensive accessories to accumulate when compared with the cost of a dress. If you will keep an eye on the fashion magazines, you can stay aware of what style shoes go with what dresses or pants, and whether such whimsies as little silk violets are in style this season. Accessories can give a great new look to last year's classics.

Now that you are slender, stylishly dressed and tastefully accessorized, don't make the mistake of ruining your new look by slouching or shuffling your feet. Stand up straight! You'll make a much more exciting entrance if you will hold your head up, smile, keep your shoulders straight and place one foot firmly in front of the other.

Just as an experiment, stand with your heels, buttocks and head against a wall and feel what "standing straight" really means. Of course, no one walks that erectly, but it is a good way to call your attention to your posture. Next time you are shopping for those just-right jackets and accessories, practice walking along the line in the sidewalk.

Cleanliness is of primary importance in looking and feeling stylish. If a problem of body odor or bad breath should persist despite your efforts to eliminate it, bear in mind two possibilities: Body odor is frequently an emotional reaction caused by nerves or stress. And bad breath can be caused by unhealthy teeth or gums, as well as by the usual culprits, onion and garlic.

To continue the "total" person look, let's be sure that your makeup is updated and designed for your particular lifestyle. Makeup seems to be a problem to a lot of women. They either don't know how to apply it properly or they are afraid to wear it at all. But when applied correctly, a little makeup can perk up nearly any face.

Clean skin is the first step toward a pretty face. Next, apply a moisturizer if you like to use one. A good moisturizer or emollient can soften character lines.

One of the main purposes for foundation, which is the next step, is to smooth out the look of the skin, disguise broken capillaries and tiny flaws, cover blemishes. Be sure to pick a color which blends closely with your skin, then blend it carefully at your chinline, not *too* far down the neck. If you have oily skin, a light dusting of translucent face powder will cut down excessive shine. Some women, however, prefer a glossy, glowing unpowdered look.

Cheek color, blush or rouge, can give your face an extra glow, whether you wear foundation makeup or not. Avoid too-bright shades; stay with the most natural-looking tones.

My personal taste is a tonal coordination between blush, lip color and nail color. Wine nail polish and orange lipstick don't work well together at all!

Your eyes may be the most important feature of your face. "Mirrors of the soul," eyes have been called. What can you do to accent your eyes? Heavy "beetle" brows can give a harsh look to an otherwise pretty face. Pluck out the extra hairs across the bridge of your nose, between your eyebrows. If you do more plucking, always pluck beneath your brow, never above.

Eyeshadow is best used, for daytime wear, as a contour rather than a color accent. Choose a soft brown, grey or rust tone, as natural as possible. A frosty touch of sparkle under your outer eyebrow will make your eyes appear larger.

Eyeliner should be applied carefully and sparingly and black should be avoided unless you have very dark skin and hair. You will want to try to be neat when you apply your eyeliner. Nothing looks worse than wiggly lines that ring your eyes uncertainly.

Perhaps the most eye-opening makeup technique today is the skillful use of mascara. My usual suggestion is that you stay with black or brown colors for daytime. Take lots of time to apply your mascara. Don't be afraid to apply a lot; just keep your eyelashes separated and try not to blob it on in great masses. And don't forget your lower lashes. Your eyes will be as bright as the person who lives behind them!

With these basics in mind, let's talk about a specific "working woman" problem: You're late. You glance in the mirror on your way out the door and your face is totally invisible! Help! You only have a couple of minutes. What do you do? What's most important?

Barring the existence of blemishes which require a little covering up, I would suggest mascara, blush and a touch of lipstick or lip gloss as the three things that will improve your looks the most the fastest. And if you're *really* late, put your mascara on at home and if you're lucky you can rouge and lipstick yourself on the way. Just don't wreck the car! But whatever you do, don't try to put mascara on in a moving auto, bus or train.

Hair is like a frame around your face; it can make a big difference in the way your face looks. What is the most important word about hair? CLEAN! And next in importance is being sure it is well conditioned. If you use electric rollers or a blow dryer, you probably should use an instant conditioner on your hair at least once a week to keep it healthy, bright and shiny.

We've all heard the guidelines about face shape and hairstyles. You can probably tell by looking what makes your face look its best. Work with your hair to determine the best style for you. If your hair is naturally curly, you're probably better off working with the curl and being thankful for it than you would be in trying to straighten it. And those of us with naturally straight hair should probably avoid tight, curly permanents. Unless a person can afford the luxury of continual professional care, permanents can be very dangerous things!

Hands, especially since so many of us use them to express ourselves when we are talking, are a vital part of an attractive total appearance. Fingernails should be kept a uniform length. Keep the cuticle neat, the polish unchipped and the shape gently rounded. Choose a nail color that blends with your lipstick and cheek tones and keep it fresh and shiny with a top coat of clear polish.

A good tip for the working woman is this: If you don't have time to keep your nails neatly polished, stick to clear gloss. That way if it's chipped, it's not obvious at a glance.

Now that we have made some suggestions on

cosmetic improvements for your outward appearance, let's focus on the *real* source of outward beauty—what's on the inside. Physically, emotionally and spiritually, your inner self is a lot more important than your outward appearance, and problems in any of the three areas can alter your outward appearance considerably.

If your physical health is not tops, it will almost always show on the outside. Circles under your eyes, bad color, blotchy skin, and dull hair and eyes can all be caused by poor health. And, of course, emotional strain will take its toll, too.

But what does spiritual well-being have to do with your looks? Aren't there a lot of beautiful girls who care nothing for things of the spirit? Of course. But joy is the greatest beautifier of all. Joy's most obvious reflection is a pretty smile. And real, deep joy comes from the innermost part of your being.

If our relationship with God is not what it should be, our spirit is out of tune and our emotional life will suffer. Even our physical health can be impaired by a spiritual imbalance. All of these imbalances will manifest themselves in our outward appearance.

And let not your adornment be external only—braiding the hair, and wearing gold jewelry, and putting on dresses; but let it be the hidden person of the heart, with the imperishable quality of a gentle and quiet spirit, which is precious in the sight of God (I Peter 3:3, 4).

As an example of the spiritual upsetting the emotional, I find I am often subject to nervousness. And in my case, nervousness creates fear—fear of physical illness, of tragedy, of the unknown. If I allow my everyday circumstances to get the best of me— something that happens when I am not trusting God with every area of my life—I become nervous. Next, I grow irritable with others. This is followed by sleeplessness, shortness of breath, heart palpitations, and eventually, terror. I end up looking as bad as I feel.

How does it start? It starts when I worry about my life and don't commit it to God.

Trust in the Lord with all thine heart; and lean not unto thine own understanding. In all thy ways acknowledge him, and he will direct thy paths (Proverbs 3:5, 6 KJV).

We are total people—in no way can we divorce our state of mind from the way we look. When we have been reborn in the Spirit of God, we have a spiritual dimension that is irreversibly bound to our emotions and our health.

But the Lord said to Samuel, "Do not look at his appearance or at the height of his stature, because I have rejected him; for God sees not as man sees, for man looks at the outward appearance, but the Lord looks at the heart (I Samuel 16:7).

This verse brings to mind another facet of personal appearance and self-concept that affects a lot of people, Christian and non-Christian alike. It has happened to me at times, and perhaps it has happened to you, too.

Sometimes when we feel plain or fat or just out-of-it, it is really something on the inside that's bothering us. We don't like our inner selves, and instead of remedying the real problem, we start trying to alter things on the outside.

When I was modeling, I worked in a spacious, old-fashioned room with a big window that overlooked Wilshire Boulevard in downtown Los Angeles. Each model had a key to the room, a mirror and a drawer for her personal use. If we worked every day, we painted our names on our mirrors with nail polish so the part-time girls would know that it was "our place." I have a mental picture of that room as a glamourous, romantic setting where we all played out our roles in a fantasy world.

But another picture remains in my mind as well. Several of the models with whom I worked would sit, day after day, staring into their mirrors, searching their faces for flaws. They would exchange the names and phone numbers of prestigious Beverly Hills plastic surgeons. And every once in awhile, one of them would be gone for a few weeks, returning with a new nose, a freshly sanded complexion, or a de-wrinkled chin. She would feel like a "new woman" for a week or two, then would begin to search the mirror again.

One particular woman, who underwent several

surgeries in the time I was there, talked to me about her life. She felt hollow and empty. Her marriage was a disaster. She was terrified of the future, when she would be old and her beauty would be gone. Since she didn't really like the person she knew so well on the inside, she kept trying to change the face she saw on the outside. And yet, sad as it was, she continued to reject Jesus because she couldn't bear to give up the control she thought she had over her destiny!

Most of us care greatly about our outward appearance. And because we care about it, God cares about it too, because He loves us. And God knows, too, that it is far more difficult for us to be His lights to the world if we are so self-conscious that we are unable to speak about Him. He will help every one of us with our appearance if our motives are right, if we really want to serve Him.

But let's be sure to start at the beginning. Let's give God the innermost part of our being and let Him beautify that. Let's confess our faults to one another and to Him, freeing ourselves from guilt. Let's surrender our circumstances to God so that we have nothing to worry about.

Then, when those basics are taken care of, let's start on the outside, beautifying the temple of God, doing our best to make it a place that reflects Him—a home for the Spirit.

Lord . . .
Grant me inner beauty,
And teach me outward beauty.

Not that I may outshine others,
But that I may be totally and completely
Transformed by your love.
Most of all,
Let the beauty of Jesus
Be seen in me.

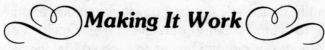

Making It Work

1. What are the things you like best about your looks? List them and thank God for them.
2. What are the things about your appearance that you wish were different?
   a. Write them down, then put a check by the things you *cannot* change. Pray that God will help you to accept and to be thankful for those things.
   b. After listing the things you *can* change, set a date/goal for yourself. Ask God to help you improve yourself in those areas by the date that you've set.

3
Wednesday
Why Can't We
Get Along?

The day dawned hot and still. By noon the temperature had soared to nearly 100 degrees. Everyone in the room felt sticky and limp for, despite the building's cooling system, there was no escape from the stifling weather.

The two women had never been great friends at the office, for Rose often seemed to be hostile and argumentative. So today when Rose snapped at her it came as no surprise. Rose was older than she and had worked for the company longer. She had been passed over for the last promotion—something she never mentioned but which was obviously an irritation to her.

Today, however, Debby was not as even-tempered as she had been in the past. When Rose's voice level rose and her tone became derisive, Debby felt a surge of temper that she hadn't experienced in years. Her face grew red. Her fists clenched. She whirled and faced Rose.

"I'm sick of you!" she began. "I'm tired of your arrogance and your criticism. Why don't you just shut up and keep your nose out of my work!" She continued to speak, her words clipped, her eyes angry.

After the scene was over, Debby could remember little of what she had said. She felt tired and shaken and just a little sad. Rose had left the room in great haste and, as she sat alone she wondered, "Why do these things happen? Why can't we get along?"

One of the most exasperating situations that can happen to a working woman is a personality conflict. It takes more energy and causes more worry than virtually any other circumstance that exists. And the worst of it is—it happens almost every day to one of us. Sometimes it is the boss. Sometimes it is a co-worker. But whoever, the problem is one that exists and must be faced.

An easy Christian platitude for such problems is, "Just love them in the Lord." Of course God's love is a gift to us as Christians, and we need only appropriate it in order to let it flow through us and touch those with whom we come in contact.

But like it or not, ideal or not, there are going to be individuals we don't understand, whom we don't get along with—that we, in honest terms, don't like. It isn't God's plan that we feel this way. But until we are perfected or at least become very mature Christians, let's face facts: Personality conflicts exist, and we need to try to understand our reactions in order to cope with them intelligently.

So . . . what causes personality problems? Let's start with you. How do you appear to others? Are you moody? Even-tempered? Neat? Messy? Strong-willed? Gentle? Prompt? Unconcerned with time? Confident? Insecure? Pretty? Plain?

Just about every quality that you or I exhibit is a potential threat to someone else. If the person we face is uncertain about himself in any area, our strength in that area can become an irritation to him, without our having any control over it. This is one source of trouble.

Another problem area is *our* feelings about the person and how we respond to *his* idiosyncracies. I'm thinking of two chronically organized people whom I know pretty well. Both compartmentalize everything from postage stamps to pencils, facing all their dollar bills the same direction, keeping neatly printed little lists of things to do.

One of these men is a personal friend for whom I have a great deal of respect. I am aware of his habits, but they don't annoy me in any way. The other man is an ex-boss of mine with whom I had little in common. All the time I worked for him I had a fiendish desire to unstraighten the papers on his desk or to pour his paper clips on the floor. He drove me crazy with his neatness.

Because I loved the first person, I accepted him as he was. Without emotional love for the second man, I could not overlook what I considered his "flaw." (He, naturally, thought his neatness was a virtue!)

It is sometimes easy for a Christian to take for granted the security and peace of mind that the Father gives to His children. When we have been Christians for awhile, we can grow callous to the needs of others. We forget the struggles the world faces outside Christ. If we will put ourselves, through imagination, in the other person's place, we may better understand him. What are his needs? What has he been through in his life? What is he going through right now? What makes him act the way he does? What can I do to alleviate his fear or to make him feel cared for and secure?

Many people are tormented by fear and failure. They have no hope that the future will be better than the past. They struggle to attain some kind of self-reliance that will help them through life. Perhaps we have a tendency to grow impatient with these people. We say, "They've heard the Answer and have rejected Him so the rest is their hard luck." Let's try to remember that one of the fruits of God's Spirit is patience. God hasn't given up on these people. And He hasn't told us to grow weary of their woes.

What He *has* told us is to love them. To hurt with them. To share their burdens, lending a concerned ear and a willing shoulder. Judging non-Christians (or even fellow Christians) is *never* our responsibility.

When we have taken into consideration the problems that another person is facing, it is far easier for us to accept him as he is, forgiving him his foibles. But what if there is something about a person that is more than you can bear? When, no matter how you try to rationalize it, you just can't abide something that he does?

I once worked with a woman who, from time to time, lapsed into a kind of baby-talk when she was attempting to be cute. She was well into her forties and the effect was less than flattering. She was also prone to door-slamming and fits of tears at the slightest provocation. Oh, how she irritated me!

One night I went home, feeling deeply convicted about my bad attitude. I attempted to put into writing the things she did that bothered me and why they made me react so negatively. I worked for hours, solving and resolving the circumstance. I came up with some sort of conclusion that she was insulting my intelligence by playacting, and I was too proud to accept her various roles. It was a lovely conclusion. Unfortunately, she bothered me just as much the next day!

At last, someone in our office, a non-Christian who was probably more kindhearted than I in the long run, took the lady aside and told her that she was really annoying everyone. The woman was unaware that she was annoying *anyone,* and after the initial hurt wore off, she "grew up" a little—there was a noticeable improvement in her personality.

All my introspection may have tickled my intellect somewhat, but it did little to resolve the situation. There are times when a word tactfully spoken can make a great difference. It is always a good idea to examine our motives, of course. However, in spite of whether the truth hurts, it can really heal.

Wednesday: Why Can't We Get Along?

Have you ever come in contact with a person who is pushy, blustering and nearly always on the defensive? This sort of person is quick to jump on your failings, quicker to defend himself and to put the blame on you. He may be perfectly friendly during coffee time, then turn on you the moment a work-related question arises.

Did you know that these individuals are often very insecure and highly sensitive? They have formed hard crusts to protect themselves and often depend on their work to give them respectability and a "place" in the world. That doesn't mean that they aren't troublesome! But it means that we can, if we will, understand and love them a little more easily.

Another type of person you're sure to meet along the workworld road is the heavy competitor. This sort of person always seems to be in some sort of race to the top. He will at least mildly resent your successes, and will always do his part in letting his virtues be known to all who will listen.

If you have a competitive streak yourself, you may find it easy to slip into this pattern, too—joining in the footrace, proving your own worth. I can't say what this individual's motives are. He, too, may be seeking recognition to fill a void. He may be on a make-money-quick campaign. Whatever the reason, let him pass you. God is looking out for your success and your financial security. If you're doing your best, relax and don't worry about the "ladder." Let God take care of it.

Then there is the unfortunate one who has been

promoted beyond his capabilities. This sad situation often happens to the conscientious, deserving individual who has faithfully done his job for a long time. When he is given bigger responsibilities, he sometimes is in over his head, desperately trying to find his way. It might be wise for him to try to go back to something he can handle, but the truth is, he's scared. He has learned to depend on the additional salary and he is afraid that if he admits he is not making it, he'll completely lose his job. Be patient with him. It could happen to you! And if it should, by all means tell the truth. And let the Lord work out the details.

About the time I began to write this book, I received the biggest promotion I had ever had. I went from being an "underling" to having a handful of people under me. And two things were made evident to me in that situation.

First, I had no control over my promotion. Before I was promoted, I thought I was forever lodged in a position from which there was no apparent escape, in a company where there were twice as many people as there needed to be. In the next job higher for which I was most qualified, there were four people in the way, all of whom had been with the company longer than I. I was stuck, or so it seemed.

But new management arrived. Overstaffing was cut. People were transferred from one department to another without a day's notice. Within a week I was in a new job, better than any I had ever had, making more money than I had ever made. I found out later that three people had given the new general manager my resume without my knowledge. He had created a position for me. At least *he* thought he had. But the truth is, God put me where He wanted me for a time, using others to accomplish His purpose.

The second thing I learned is that it isn't *easy* to go from being *under* people to being *over* them. I have encountered varying forms of resentment, beginning with "She has changed" to "I should have had the job, not her," and ending with "Don't tell me what to do."

How can Christian principles be exercised in this type of situation? Jesus told His people to be servants to all—and if you are the "boss," that instruction creates a peculiar dilemma. How can you be a servant and a master at the same time? I believe the answer lies in the very essence of Jesus' teaching. It is the *spirit* of servitude that He was talking about—not thinking that we're above doing anything, not thinking that we are better than the person doing the lesser task. When we ask an employee to do something for us, our attitude needs to be loving and unintimidating. My job, as a supervisor, is to bring out the very best, through love, in every person whom I direct.

Beloved, let us love one another, for love is from God; and every one who loves is born of God and knows God. The one who does not love does not know God, for God is love. By this the love of God was manifested in us, that God has sent His only begotten Son into the world so that we might live through Him.

In this is love, not that we loved God, but that He loved us and sent His Son to be the propitiation for our sins. Beloved, if God so loved us, we also ought to love one another (I John 4:7-11).

When asked, "What commandment is the foremost of all?" Jesus Himself said:

"The foremost is, 'Hear, O Israel; The Lord our God is one Lord; and you shall love the Lord your God with all your heart, and with all your soul, and with all your mind, and with all your strength.'

"The second is this, 'You shall love your neighbor as yourself.' There is no other commandment greater than these" (Mark 12:28-31).

In my experience, the most important concept to keep in mind at work, at home or wherever is that love is a *principle,* and more than just an emotion. Treating people with love is a discipline, just like not losing your temper or keeping your mind on the job.

Love is patient, love is kind, and is not jealous; love does not brag and is not arrogant, does not act unbecomingly; it does not seek its own, is not provoked, does not take into account a wrong suffered, does not rejoice in unrighteousness, but rejoices with the truth; bears all things, believes all things, hopes all things, endures all things (I Corinthians 13:4-7).

You may not always *feel* like loving someone. But you teach yourself not to think the worst about everything your fellow employee does, not to make those cutting remarks, not to talk about him behind his back. Gossip is one of the most harmful, damaging things that exists in the world. It disguises itself as a harmless pastime. It makes itself appear to be a typical little "feminine" trait. It causes us to feel important, able to look down on other people at the stroke of a word.

Yet some Christians don't seem too concerned about what the Bible says in regard to controlling what we say about other people.

So also the tongue is a small part of the body, and yet it boasts of great things. Behold, how great a forest is set aflame by such a small fire! And the tongue is a fire, the very world of iniquity. The tongue is set among our members as that which defiles the entire body, and sets on fire the course of our life, and is set on fire by hell.

With it we bless our Lord and Father; and with it we curse men, who have been made in the likeness of God; from the same mouth come both blessing and cursing. My brethren, these things ought not to be this way (James 3:5, 6, 9, 10).

How many times have you been in this situation? Something happens at the office—something you observe but don't take too seriously. Then . . . you go to coffee with the girls. They start talking about the circumstances and before you know it a huge crisis has arisen. Inevitably someone gets hurt.

I have been both the one hurt and the one who does the damage. And I have come to the conclusion that gossip is one of the most vicious tools that Satan has in the church today, and certainly in the world.

Do not judge lest you be judged yourselves. For in the way you judge, you will be judged; and by your standard of measure, it shall be measured to you (Matthew 7:1, 2).

For just as the body without the spirit is dead, so also faith without works is dead (James 2:26).

Judging people is a companion to gossip, and is another reason why we should avoid gossip. We all judge people daily. We make value judgments about them based on the way they dress and speak, how they act and with whom they associate. Some of these judgments can in fact help us to determine whether a person knows Jesus, but these are not infallible rules. And it is not our place, in any case, to decide a person's spiritual state, except as the Lord reveals it to us for His purposes. We are to be lights, shedding His love on all who cross our path, regardless of their position in Him. We are mirrors of Him. He told us not to judge. Let's try to remember!

Putting pride in its proper place is a good way to help control our temper and our tongue. How often we fly off the handle because our reputation, our position, or our self-righteousness is at stake. Paul said: "For through the grace given to me I say to every man among you not to think more highly of himself than he ought to think; but to think so as to have sound judgment, as God has allotted to each a measure of faith" (Romans 12:3).

Not long ago, a fashion director for whom I had worked thirteen years before came to our store to visit the president of the company. I was quite young when I had worked for her. It was one of my first jobs, as a no-shorthand secretary. Admittedly, I have never been a great secretary, and I wasn't outstanding then, but I had tried to learn and had left in good graces, or so I thought! Today I hold the woman's position in our store, so my years of work had moved me along sufficiently to where I felt that we were on somewhat the same professional level.

Through another person, word got back to me that the woman had told our president that I was the worst secretary she had ever had. All I ever did was write poetry (not altogether true). The president reportedly told her that if *he* had to be her secretary, he'd write poetry, too.

I was furious! How dare she say such a thing? I fumed and fussed for two days—almost writing her a scorching letter. She hadn't threatened my job, really. What had she done to me that was deserving of such wrath? Very simple—she had hurt my pride!

I have found prayer to be a most useful deterrent to boastful pride and anger. If you and I could only remember to pray every time we have an angry thought about another person! To pray when we feel cheated or wronged or misunderstood. If we could just divert our energies from negative emotions to constructive spiritual efforts. God is love. He is living within us. We needn't ask for more love, but rather to appropriate what already is the very nature of His Holy Spirit, what already is in us.

So let's turn over a new leaf. Let's look at ourselves objectively, as others see us. Then let's look at them as they see themselves, putting ourselves in "their shoes." Let's try to relate to their insecurities. To their needs for success. To their lack of capabilities and corresponding fears. Let's put aside gossip and self-pride.

Instead, we should allow God to work through us, allow His love to flow like a beautiful shining river, pouring over everyone who comes our way. And let's pray, first confessing our own failings to each other and to God. Then let's truly forgive the weaknesses and sins of others, always remembering—*there but for the grace of God go I.* We have Someone to bear our burdens. The non-Christian doesn't.

Wednesday: Why Can't We Get Along?

Father,
How I thank you for the freedom You have given me
From fear,
*   From anger,*
*   From hate.*
Remind me, Lord, to let You work through me.
And to love, Lord Jesus,
Not of myself
But through You.

Making It Work

1. Write the names of each co-worker with whom you have a personality conflict or a difficult time getting along.
   a. After each name list all the reasons you can think of for the problem.
   b. Pray daily for each person, asking God to help you understand him and love him.
   c. If you owe anyone on your list an apology, ask God to help you make it, sincerely and willingly.
2. List your personality traits, good and bad. Think about the kind of person you are and how you affect other people. Ask God to help you to see and to smooth out the rough spots in your personality.

4
Thursday
Lunch, Anyone?

Never before in Julie's recollection had the entire advertising staff decided to have lunch together—no bosses invited. The little group walked into the dimly lit Mexican restaurant, and with a feeling of great freedom, seated themselves at the table which had been reserved for them. The white linen napkins were folded expertly, and the crystal and silver shone.

From the time the others had first asked her to join them, Julie hadn't really been sure she wanted to go. But the whole office staff was celebrating a successful ad campaign, and she had had a big part in it.

She often went to lunch with one or two of them at a time, so she reasoned hopefully, the more the merrier! She knew the others would order drinks before lunch. That was, in part, their idea of a celebration. But they knew she didn't drink, so that was no problem.

Soon after the drinks were served, the conversation

egan to change. It grew louder. Everyone started to
laugh a lot, although nothing seemed as hilarious to
er as it did to them. Negative talk about their absent
bosses increased, as did slightly dirty jokes.

Although no one was intentionally leaving Julie out
of things, she began to feel more and more like an
outsider. She wished she were someplace else. As a
Christian, she did not want to be sitting with a group of
loud and silly people. But since she couldn't get up and
leave without making a scene, she sat quietly and
began to think very carefully. What could she say or do
to change the way things were going? Why had she
come in the first place? Would it have been better to
say, "No, thanks" when the others had asked, "Lunch,
anyone?"

In one way or another, we have all been trapped in a
situation that wasn't right for us, doing things we didn't
want to do in a group of people with whom we didn't
feel we belonged. We have all heard sermons on being
non-conforming Christians, not going along with the
crowd. And yet on occasion, we have wound up right
where we didn't mean to be at all.

Is it wrong to associate closely with those who might
cause us to compromise our principles? Or is it wrong
to avoid a situation which might prove embarrassing
and difficult? Have you ever wondered what a
Christian should do?

After much soul-searching on the subject, and after
much seeking to understand God's Word, I have come
to this conclusion: *Motivation* is the underlying

indicator of what is right and what is wrong in these difficult circumstances. *Why* are you going? Because you are afraid not to? Because you really would like to experience some of the adventures that you've heard your non-Christian friends talk about? Because you think your presence at the occasion might be an influence for the Lord? Or because you simply want to be with your friends?

Or, why *don't* you want to go? Because you feel that God doesn't want you to? Because you're afraid you'll be laughed at for not taking part in things? Because you wouldn't enjoy yourself? Because you might be tempted? Determining your motivation will help you make the correct decision.

Behold, Thou dost desire truth in the innermost being (Psalms 51:6).

In our determination of our interpersonal motivation, let's take a look at several "social activities" that Christians need to consider the rightness or wrongness of for themselves. The most obvious are smoking, drinking and drug use. Profanity, gossip, dirty jokes and complaining are other things that tend to manifest themselves in social situations.

We know that tobacco is harmful to the body—science has pretty well made that clear. Most doctors will encourage their patients to stop smoking because of possible heart and respiratory diseases. A Christian believes that his body is God's "temple," and that it should be cared for as such. Because of this, most

Christians avoid the use of tobacco.

Do you smoke? Have you thought about why? If you have a habit that goes back many years, it may seem virtually impossible for you to stop. God understands this and He will help you with your problem. He knows your emotional make-up and your needs. And because He knows what is best for you, He will provide you with the strength to quit. It may not happen overnight, but don't be discouraged. He has promised to watch over you and to help you with all your problems.

Why do people drink? Is it to escape? Is it to show off? Is it because they enjoy an occasional glass of wine with dinner and see no reason to stop having it? Or is it because they *can't* stop? The national statistics on alcoholism are staggering, so staggering that many people, including many Christians, flatly state that it is better to completely avoid the use of alcohol than to take a chance on addiction or drunkenness.

If you don't drink, this is probably another reason why you choose not to:

And do not get drunk with wine, for that is dissipation, but be filled with the Spirit (Ephesians 5:18).

But suppose you do have a drinking problem. Will God help you? Of course He will! Let's never be afraid to admit our weaknesses to God. He already knows about them. He is the Great Physician. Seek His help and also professional help if you need it. Trust God to heal you. He will!

Drugs, if they are used to alter the senses, appear to fit into the same category as being drunk, not Spirit-filled. A Christian who walks in the wonderful fullness of God's love doesn't need drugs to expand his consciousness. Life in the Spirit is as expansive an experience as anyone can ever know. But again, if you need help with drugs, find a Christian drug counseling organization and let them, with God's help, help you solve your problem.

A Christian concept which cannot be ignored in discussing controversial social activities is that of not "offending the brethren." Just what does this mean? In our day and age, most of us have the attitude of "live and let live." And yet the Bible tells us that we *should* be concerned with what other believers think of us. This can be difficult—but what it really amounts to is another way of acting out Christian love. If you or I really love another person, we don't want to irritate him or cause him grief by tempting him to do something that he doesn't feel is right. It is not that we are afraid of what he says about us; instead, we are concerned about his spiritual health.

For through your knowledge he who is weak is ruined, the brother for whose sake Christ died. And thus, by sinning against the brethren and wounding their conscience when it is weak, you sin against Christ. Therefore, if food causes my brother to stumble, I will never eat meat again, that I might not cause my brother to stumble (I Corinthians 8:11-13).

Profanity is a good example of this. While most Christians avoid taking the Lord's name in vain, there are other words which are simply crude or vulgar. Other "swear words" may be right on the borderline— we may see no great harm in using them. But if such words offend other Christians, we should, out of consideration, remove them from our vocabularies.

Sometimes there are ways, far less obvious than profanity, by which we can offend other Christians. A few years ago long hair, beards and sideburns meant "hippie" or "drug addict" to a lot of people. My dad, a pillar of his church, a man of prayer, and an arch-conservative himself, had sideburns that reached, *maybe*, to the bottom of his ears. An acquaintance of his, also a Christian, told Daddy that his sideburns were an offense to him and he should shave them off. So, without too much consideration, Daddy shaved his sideburns.

When I heard this some months later, I was so annoyed with the man that I could hardly listen to the story! How narrow-minded could anyone be? How could anyone be offended by a sixty-five year old Baptist church deacon with two-and-a-half inch sideburns? Grey sideburns!

But Daddy had the right idea. He handled the situation in love, not in rebellion. And rather than argue or debate the matter, he acted as a Christian brother should act. The truth is, I am still not sure in similar circumstances I would be as kind a Christian. Nevertheless, that's what maturity is all about, isn't it?

Naturally, it's impossible to please every Christian.

There are times when demands may be made on us by fellow believers which are unnecessary, unreasonable or irrational. We need to ask God for wisdom when this happens.

> But if any of you lacks wisdom, let him ask of God, who gives to all men generously and without reproach, and it will be given to him (James 1:5).

Some of us Christians who have made up our minds about drinking, smoking and such vices are sometimes quick to criticize: "Well, he DRINKS, you know." Or, "Is she a Christian? I doubt it, she SMOKES." (Christians are seldom so quick to react to overeating and unsafe driving!) The fact is, *we are not given the responsibility for such judging of one another.* Let's not make value judgments based on external evidence. God looks at the heart. He works in each of our lives in a different way, at a different pace. And He deeply loves each of us, faults included.

> But you, why do you judge your brother? Or you again, why do you regard your brother with contempt? For we shall all stand before the judgment seat of God.

> For it is written, "As I live, says the Lord, every knee shall bow to Me, and every tongue shall give praise to God." So then each one of us shall give account of himself to God.

Therefore, let us not judge one another any more, but rather determine this—not to put an obstacle or a stumbling block in a brother's way (Romans 14:10-13).

As I stated earlier, related closely to judging is gossiping. For when we have made the judgment, we are prone to verbalize it, especially about those not present. We work side by side with people every day, see them at their best and their worst, learn about their personal lives, notice the way they dress. What a wonderland of juicy tidbits it provides us with when they aren't around to defend themselves!

What does God think? "For we all stumble in many ways. If any one does not stumble in what he says, he is a perfect man, able to bridle the whole body as well" (James 3:2).

In recent years I have noticed something terrifying about gossip. Lives are affected by it. It is not at all an innocent pastime. People are swayed—minds are changed by conversations. Every time you or I say something ill about someone, we place a negative thought in the mind of another. When such thoughts are passed on to the wrong people, which is what usually happens, reputations can be ruined, jobs can be lost, marriages can be damaged, friendships can be destroyed. This is not "idle" chatter.

What *is* it about gossip that is so appealing to so many of us? Two or three things come to my mind when I try to sort out my own failings in this area.

Most obvious is the desire to lift ourselves above

another person. By criticizing or finding fault with others, we immediately have the feeling that we have elevated ourselves to a more lofty position than theirs. In essence, we are trying to create the impression that they are answerable to us, that they owe us an explanation for their behavior. And *we* wish to appear, in our own eyes and hopefully in the eyes of those listening, far "better" people than they.

Another factor in the problem of gossip is the "inside information" syndrome. Being able to "scoop" everybody with a story can be a nearly insurmountable temptation. It shows that we were chosen as worthy hearers of a prize tale. We were closer to the source than the persons to our immediate left and right. Doesn't that prove how wonderful we are?

A third gossip motivation is our human desire to be a part of the conversation. Sometimes it just simply boils down to this: do we sit at the table like a lump and say nothing or do we contribute a little to the conversation and prove that we are aware and opinionated, too?

Beware of the Christian subterfuge tactic: "I'm just telling you this because I know you'll want to pray for poor old sinful Susie." I'm sure there are other reasons for gossip besides these, but suffice it to say, all these things are unworthy motives for character assassination!

Dirty jokes offend many Christians. Christians should avoid them, although we can't always avoid hearing them. But passing them on is another matter; we can avoid that!

How should one react to these stories? People

handle the problem in varying ways—from pretending not to understand, to ignoring the entire story, to saying "shame on you," to actually stating that they are offended. Choose the method that suits you best, keeping in mind a spirit of love and tactfulness.

Let no unwholesome word proceed from your mouth, but only such a word as is good for edification according to the need of the moment, that it may give grace to those who hear (Ephesians 4:29).

But do not let immorality or any impurity or greed even be named among you, as is proper among saints; and there must be no filthiness and silly talk, or coarse jesting, which are not fitting, but rather giving of thanks (Ephesians 5:3, 4).

Before I gave my life to the Lord, a teacher told me that I was the most negative person he had ever met. Believe me, I wasn't cured overnight, but God has taught me something, based on these scriptural facts:

Always giving thanks for all things in the name of our Lord Jesus Christ to God, even the Father (Ephesians 5:20).

For it is God who is at work in you, both to will and to work for His good pleasure. Do all things without grumbling or disputing; that you may prove yourselves to be blameless and innocent, children of God above reproach in the midst of a crooked and perverse generation, among whom you appear as lights in the world, holding fast the word of life (Philippians 2:13-16).

It's a simple premise. When something doesn't please you, thank God for it. First of all, He has allowed it to be in your life for a purpose. And secondly, He has promised to work it out for good. He loves you so much!

Well . . . so far, the lunch party hasn't been much fun, has it? So let's look at it another way and see what God can do with a difficult situation, how He can make it pleasant and good. As we talked about in the first chapter, we are put where we are to be lights to the world. A sweet spirit, a friendly smile and an understanding ear can do more to add a positive dimension to a "worldly" party than all the scowls and sermonettes in the world.

If the conversation starts getting muddy, tactfully change the subject. If someone starts tearing another person apart, gently insert something good about the absent individual. Be kind. Complimentary. Positive. Friendly. In that way, your presence at a company lunch can change the mood of the entire occasion from typical to enjoyable. And you won't leave feeling tainted or guilty, either. Remember, wherever you go, the Lord goes with you. Let His light shine!

It is important to think about how our lives affect other Christians, but how about our unbelieving friends? What do they see in us as Christians? In my experience with non-Christians, they are a lot more impressed with a loving spirit than with a person who observes a lot of do's and don'ts.

A "Christian" person is sometimes described as one who "never says a bad word about anyone," who "is always there when you need him," or who "has a really positive attitude." Does this describe us? Even if it does, it still is not enough just to be on our best behavior. We have got to let people know *why* we are the way we are.

I have a friend who is absolutely beautiful, inside and out. She is lovely to look at. She doesn't smoke, seldom swears, never drinks too much. She doesn't gossip, always has something nice to say, always encourages me when I'm down.

She is a faithful wife, a concerned and loving mother and a precious friend. And although she does not believe in Jesus as anyone other than a "good" man and an example, in action she probably appears to be more of a real Christian than I do!

My point is this: Our behavior is very important. But a verbal explanation of our way of life somewhere along the line is essential so that others will know "why" and not just "what." Naturally, the risks are greater if we let people know we're Christians. They will expect a great deal more of us. But always remember—the world is full of really "good" people. *We* are more than good. We are reborn spiritually— with a future hope as well as a present behavior pattern. Let's explain ourselves!

All things must pass, and at last the lunch party's over. What do we do if we've blown it? What if we found ourselves backstabbing someone who wasn't there? Or telling dirty stories? Or complaining? What should we do?

If we confess our sins, He is faithful and righteous to forgive us our sins and to cleanse us from all unrighteousness (I John 1:9).

Go to God, as we all have to do every day, and tell Him what you've done wrong. Perhaps, in addition, talk it over with a Christian friend. But make up your mind that you really don't want to make the same mistakes again. Repenting—turning from—is part of confession. We need to make an honest effort not to commit that sin again.

No condemnation now hangs over the head of those who are in Christ Jesus (Romans 8:1).

Forgiveness is that simple. You have no reason for further guilt. When you are forgiven, God sees you as perfect as Jesus Himself.

Perhaps you have nothing to feel guilty about. Perhaps you behaved the way you wanted to at the lunch party. Were you laughed at for your good conduct? Occasionally, we all will experience outright persecution. What should our reaction be?

Here is some scripture that talks pretty plainly

about our attitude toward the "world" under these circumstances:

Bless those who persecute you; bless and curse not. Rejoice with those who rejoice, and weep with those who weep. Be of the same mind toward one another; do not be haughty in mind, but associate with the lowly. Do not be wise in your own estimation.

Never pay back evil for evil to anyone. Respect what is right in the sight of all men. If possible, so far as it depends on you, be at peace with all men.

Never take your own revenge, beloved, but leave room for the wrath of God, for it is written, "Vengeance is Mine, I will repay, says the Lord."

But if your enemy is hungry, feed him, and if he is thirsty, give him a drink; for in so doing you will heap burning coals upon his head. Do not be overcome by evil, but overcome evil with good (Romans 12:14-21).

Our motivations create our actions. Let's examine ourselves. By thinking through our motives, we can reach the root of our failures and we can increase our spiritual success. Then we will begin to be the people that we really want to be.

Let's ask God to help us. David's prayer in Psalms 139:23, 24 could be yours this very day!

"Search me, O God,
And know my heart;
Try me
And know my anxious thoughts;
And see if there be any hurtful way in me,
And lead me
In the everlasting way."

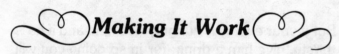

Making It Work

1. Try to remember the last "social event" that took place
   involving your co-workers.
   a. Did you go? Why? Why not?
   b. If you went, did you have a good time? Do you
      remember wishing that you'd done or said anything
      in a different way?
2. In light of God's Word, write your own "Code of Ethics"
   for socializing, keeping in mind *your* specific weaknesses. After the next office party or luncheon, check
   up on yourself. How did you do?
3. Confess your faults to God and ask Him to help you
   do better next time.

5
Friday
Why Is He
Staring At Me?

Joyce first noticed him in the teacher's room at the school where they both taught. He wasn't the best looking man she'd ever seen, but he had nice eyes and a charming way of smiling at her quickly when she looked his way. After she learned his name, she always said hello to him, and it seemed to her that he went out of his way to speak, too.

One afternoon he stopped by her classroom to ask her to coffee. She went, and the conversation, if not intoxicating, was enjoyable. They seemed to have so much in common.

Weeks went by. She was dating others, yet she looked forward to going to work a little more, knowing he was there. Once they had lunch, another day, dinner. She thought about him, forgot about him, then thought about him again.

Then, during a morning recess when she had

playground duty, she glanced upward toward a corridor and saw him standing there, smiling, watching her. Butterflies danced inside her! "What is he thinking?" she wondered, as she smiled and quickly averted her glance. *Does he really like me? Why is he staring at me?*

Ah, romance! If there has ever been anything to quicken the pulse, to get us going in the morning, to make us feel good all over, it's romance. We've grown up with stories of Prince Charming *always* coming along at the right time. Of love conquering all. Of poor little girls who marry fabulously wealthy men and live happily ever after. And every once in awhile romance knocks on the door of our lives, filling the air with magic.

What is it all about, really? What is a woman looking for in all this? What is a man looking for? Is it companionship? Friendship? Courtship? Challenge? Sex? Status? Money? The list of possibilities goes on and on.

When I was in my late teens and well into my twenties, I think I would have sold my soul for romance. I lived in a virtual fantasy world inhabited by every man I even remotely cared about. I daydreamed and wrote poetry and cried and giggled and stared and hoped. And I usually lost! Firmly believing, however, that it was "better to have loved and lost . . ." I bravely rushed into the next infatuation, casting reason to the wind.

Looking back now, I can see that in many ways I

worshiped romance; it was almost a false god to me. The hardest thing ever for me to commit to God was my love life.

Now, at the time, no one could have told me this. After all, wasn't love a virtue? And who could argue but that love made the world go around? Yet, now that I am forever with the man whom I love most in the world, I can look back and see that I wasn't as committed a Christian as I thought. In my thinking, God could have everything else; my emotions belonged to *me.*

Of course, this is not meant to say that it's wrong to be "in love." Not at all—it's *wonderful* to be in love, part of the time anyway. God uses the romances in our lives to teach us about Himself, or at least He always did with me. He taught me about waiting and trusting and healing broken hearts and yes, even about Christian commitment. And He taught me about the greatest love of all—His love for me.

In discussing romance and love, perhaps we should clarify one matter—are you married? A few years ago I would have said it doesn't really matter. Romance is *romance,* and as long as you don't actively encourage a relationship with someone other than your husband, it doesn't make any difference whether you are married. I have heard the same sort of thing from other Christians, too: "You're bound to have a crush on someone at some time after you're married—it just happens."

Since that time, however, I have seen several marriages, a few of them Christian, damaged or ended by that very philosophy. And today I feel like this: It may be natural for us to be attracted to men other than our husband after we are married, but it is not necessary to *pursue* the attraction by daydreaming and hoping and plotting. Our Lord is the Lord of our emotions, too, and He taught us when He was with us that to lust after someone is the same as committing adultery.

I don't think that most women, at least Christian women, sit around having a great many sexual fantasies. With women, fantasy is more of a romantic nature, involving "what he said to me," "how he looked at me" and "what he thinks of me." But if you are married, even the most seemingly harmless daydream sows a seed of dissatisfaction with your husband.

If allowed to grow, it can produce eventual heartbreak. A girl with whom I once modeled was a newlywed, married less than a year to a man for whom she had left her first husband. And he had left his first wife for her—they were apparently madly in love. Yet, before much time had gone by, she had heard from an old flame. Within weeks she was sexually involved with him and having serious doubts about her new marriage.

When her old flame finally dropped her, she settled down to make the best of her relationship with her husband. But guess what? *He* had suddenly become terribly infatuated with his secretary. He told his wife (who now seemed to be madly in love with him again) that he didn't love her anymore. Meanwhile, Secretary was preparing to leave *her* husband. On and on it went, marriages dissolving right and left.

These people were not Christians, but Christians are not immune to infatuation and sexual attraction. If care is not taken, the same thing can happen to a Christian couple.

My point is this: Don't allow your imagination to run away with you if you are married *or* if you are attracted to a married man. Either way it is a one way street that leads to emotional disaster.

And that brings us to our next question—is *he* married?

Have you heard the sad story yourself? His wife doesn't understand him? You are different somehow? She is cold, insensitive, unlike him, and more than that, unlike *you?* Oh, what an ego trip it is, especially if he is someone whom you admire.

If you happen to know his wife, doesn't she suddenly change before your eyes? Don't her faults become immediately apparent? Don't you wonder why he ever married her in the first place?

Please be very careful if you find yourself in this predicament, because nine and a half times out of ten you are the one who is going to be hurt. When it all comes down to the finale, he most probably is not going to leave her. But if he should do so, chances are he will grow dissatisfied with you before long, too, because the person he is really unhappy with is himself.

Whatever you do, avoid being the "other woman." It is a hopeless, thankless position. And as a Christian, it can do nothing but undermine your relationship with the Lord. Be careful of your heart!

There is another situation which I have seen happen to working women, although it has never happened to me. It could be called "sexual manipulation." Suppose your employer is attracted to you. He expects your company at lunch. Or at dinner. Or maybe he expects more than your company. You need your job, need your paycheck and you are afraid to say no.

Please remember, as a Christian, that God will supply your financial requirements. He has promised to take care of you. And He most assuredly does *not* want you to sacrifice your Christian or moral principles for your job, or for the sake of your boss's feelings. Your purity and holiness are very precious things to God.

Saying no to your boss may not be easy, but ask the Lord to help turn it into an opportunity for expressing God's love to him. Tell the man the truth—that you are a Christian, and that your life belongs to Jesus. If that makes him angry, it's unfortunate. Perhaps, instead, it will cause his respect for you to increase, and your "light" will be able to shine a little more brightly. Be tactful. Be kind. But don't allow yourself to be used.

And don't allow yourself to "use" a man by the same means. Sometimes when we are aware of the fact that a man is attracted to us, we tend to take advantage of his affections by asking him to do things for us, by allowing him to take us to lunch, by making the most of his good nature. We sometimes think that his emotional feelings are "his problem," and if he is dumb enough to do extra work or to make extra effort on our behalf, too bad! I do believe that as Christian women we have additional responsibilities to ourselves and to God to keep our standards and attitudes healthy and honest and pure. For some reason, working women are thought to be more lax in this area.

Even in today's open-minded world, a working woman is not always looked upon favorably. A woman executive recently told me she believes that many people think she is "tougher than a man" because of her position in her firm. They say she has had to be "hard" to get to the position she is in.

Little thought, she feels, is given to her qualifications or to the job she has done. And, I may add, she is not a particularly "tough" woman at all. There are many, many misconceptions about working women and we can only combat them by being real people, by being true to our faith, and by letting the Spirit of Jesus work through us, His love being our most visible attribute.

If you are single, with your whole life ahead of you, you're probably hoping that one of these days Mr. Right will appear on the horizon—and all at once the sun is going to rise when he enters the scene! Do you think that God cares about your love life? Of course He does!

No good thing does He withhold from those who walk uprightly. O Lord of hosts, How blessed is the man who trusts in Thee! (Psalms 84:11, 12).

O fear the Lord, you His saints; For to those who

fear Him, there is no want. The young lions do lack and suffer hunger; But they who seek the Lord shall not be in want of any good thing (Psalms 34:9, 10).

Delight yourself in the Lord; and He will give you the desires of your heart (Psalms 37:4).

Perhaps the biggest enemy the single girl has, Christian or not, is desperation. You're suddenly afraid that you'll spend the rest of your life alone. You feel there's something wrong with you that you can't seem to find. The "good" ones have gotten away. You're not getting any younger.

Then all at once a new man enters your life. He is not quite right somehow. He has some irritating habits. You're not as attracted to him as you would like to be, although he seems to like you. Perhaps he is financially irresponsible. Or, most difficult of all, he is not a Christian. Should you compromise? Are your goals too high? Are you growing callous and building up walls of fear? If you let him go, will he be your last living, breathing chance?

So many unhappy marriages I can think of have been born of desperation—usually that of the woman. Our upbringing, or our mothers, or movies, or love songs, or *something* has given us the idea that if we don't get married by a certain age, we are failures. This kind of desperation in a Christian girl's life can really be a serious thing because it is a symptom of not trusting the Lord.

Did you ever think about the fact that God *created* love and romance and marriage? God made you with the feelings that you have. And He will give you the desires of your heart if you trust Him.

If marriage is not in God's plan for you, He'll change your mind about wanting it. He'll show you something better. I've never yet met a dedicated Christian who felt that God had deprived him of anything. Frequently, our problem is patience—learning to wait on the Lord, accepting His timetable.

Wait for the Lord; Be strong, and let your heart take courage; yes, wait for the Lord (Psalms 27:14).

They are new every morning; Great is Thy faithfulness. "The Lord is my portion," says my soul, "Therefore I have hope in Him." The Lord is good to those who wait for Him, To the person who seeks Him (Lamentations 3:23-25).

In her refusal to accept God's timetable, to wait for the right man, the Christian woman may turn to dating non-Christians. Where does this lead? And what does the Bible say?

In my opinion, one good reason for Christians to avoid dating non-believers is self-defense. If you don't plan to spend your life with someone, why get a relationship started? Why take the chance of hurting him or yourself or both of you when you never meant for anything to come of it in the first place?

Of course you'll have lunch dates with non-

Christians at work. And there'll probably be times when you'll find yourself in the company of non-Christians during your dating life. And I can't deny that there have been circumstances where a Christian girl has led her unsaved boyfriend to God, and vice versa. But unless you are *absolutely* sure that what you are doing is in God's hands, and under His control—avoid complications!

Perhaps you don't understand why it is so important not to marry a non-Christian. Is it just an out-dated, old-fashioned idea?

I have a dear friend, a Christian, who is involved in the entertainment business and lives and works in Hollywood. She doesn't come across a great many Christian men in her line of work and often finds herself in the company of non-believers.

About a year ago she began to go out with an attractive, successful musician. Although he wasn't a Christian, he was Jewish—so he believed in God, was moral and a "good" person. At first their relationship was fine, because they felt the same way about "how" to live, and they seldom discussed their differences in belief.

Time passed, however, and as with all relationships, theirs couldn't remain static. They tentatively talked of marriage, but the more they talked, the more certain my friend became that it wouldn't work. By then, however, they had learned to care for each other a great deal, and the anguish within her was great, as well as the guilt she felt in hurting him. Here's part of a letter she wrote to me:

For nearly a year I have been attending church regularly and I praise God, because this "food" has given me the strength and sight to keep things in perspective . . . Ron knows how important Christ is to me, and accepts it, but he doesn't understand why I could (and do) feel that this difference between us confuses the relationship and makes me so unhappy at times. I realize that until *he* seeks the Lord he won't understand, at least not fully. When I tell him of my doubt and fear concerning this, there is such pain in his eyes—he is so afraid of losing me. I hope when you pray for me, that you pray for him, too.

She has since told him that they must part ways, but saying goodbye has been very, very painful.

Second Corinthians contains the only scripture that I know of specifically warning against marrying a non-believer, unless you delve into the Old Testament and find a parallel between today's Christian and yesterday's children of Israel who were most severely warned not to be united in marriage to a "heathen."

But our one New Testament verse makes a philosophical point which is the real reason for such beliefs—how can light live with darkness?

Do not be bound together with unbelievers; for what partnership have righteousness and lawlessness, or what fellowship has light with darkness? Or what harmony has Christ with Belial,

or what has a believer in common with an un-
believer? (II Corinthians 6:14, 15).

In simple words, you and he are from two different
worlds. Your value systems, your priorities, your
standards of behavior are different because they are
based on different ways of thinking. You two have
nothing on which to place the most elementary
foundations of marital understanding.

You may feel the same way about many things in the
beginning, but eventually the agreement is bound to
break down because your viewpoint is based on Christ
and His teachings, and his on some form of human
reason. God didn't give this guideline to us just to be
stern or difficult. Instead, He has our happiness in
mind.

This is not to say that you will never be swept off
your feet by a handsome, desirable man who isn't a
reborn child of God. Your emotions are still alive and
well, I imagine, but if you should become infatuated
with such a man, take it to God in prayer. He cares and
He will give you wisdom when you ask Him.

With such severe warnings against marrying a
non-believer, perhaps you are worried about your
personal situation because you are already married to
one. Here's what the Bible says to you:

And a woman who has an unbelieving husband,
and he consents to live with her, let her not send
her husband away. For the unbelieving husband
is sanctified through his wife, and the unbelieving

wife is sanctified through her believing husband; for otherwise your children are unclean, but now they are holy.

Yet if the unbelieving one leaves, let him leave; the brother or the sister is not under bondage in such cases, but God has called us to peace (I Corinthians 7:13-15).

Whatever your circumstances, please, don't stop wanting God's will for your life. Nothing is worth the sacrifice of His blessings.

Now—suppose you are dating a Christian man, someone from your church or work or wherever. And it appears to be a promising relationship but you are not sure why. Think about it.

Is it his looks—which is to say, are you physically attracted to him? That's important, to be sure, because without physical attraction, many relationships eventually crumble. (By the way—a man doesn't have to be "good" looking to be physically attractive! It's more than looks, more than style, but no one has ever yet really explained "it"!)

Or are you in love with his money? Or his money-making capacity for the future? Of course he should be able to support you, but there are no guarantees in this life except the ones that God Himself has made. To marry a man for his money is, needless to say, a grave mistake.

Is he your best friend? Oh, how important this is! If you can share yourself openly, without foolish cat-and-mouse games, if you can talk intelligently about all kinds of things, small and large, and if there's a little infatuation thrown in for good measure, you have a precious thing.

What should you be looking for? Does he bring out the best in you? Are you surprised at your patience with him? Is it easy to overlook his little faults because you are more aware of his strengths? Do you respect him? Are you happy to be alone with him, without benefit of other company? Do you share many common interests? Does he only have eyes for you? Does he really, genuinely love God?

A word to the wise—if he bugs you a lot when you're dating, he'll drive you crazy when you're married, after the honeymoon is over. If you don't really respect him, you will certainly find it hard to submit to him in love as a Christian woman should. Don't believe the story that any two Christians are "right" for each other just because they're Christians. It simply is not true.

Perhaps, after you have answered these questions honestly, you find that he is not the right man for you. How do you break off the dating relationship?

Do both your man and yourself a favor; tell him the truth. Don't try to pin your uncertainty on God unless that is the real reason. When I attended a Christian college, the standard excuse given for breaking up was something like this: "I've prayed a lot about this and I feel that it's God's will for us to test our love for awhile—apart. If it's His will for us to be together, we'll both be available after this period of testing." Translated, it meant, "There's someone else I'd *really* like to take out." Or, "I'm getting bored with you."

God should enter into your decision; that goes without saying. But don't skirt the real issues. Be honest. You and your friend will both grow from the truth.

Perhaps you've answered the questions and proven to yourself that marriage is where you're headed. It's the biggest decision you'll ever make on a human level. Never in your life will you be more in need of guidance. There are many broken lives in the world, and all of them aren't victims of divorce. Some are the lives of people who have stayed together and tried to make the marriage work, knowing full well that they have made a mistake.

Don't let that happen to you. Let God show you the way. Put Him first in your life—way up there ahead of men and dating and romance and everything else. John said it so well: "Little children, guard yourselves from idols" (I John 5:21). Romance *can* be a false god! Jesus said:

> "But seek first His kingdom and His righteous-ness; and all these things shall be added to you. Therefore do not be anxious for tomorrow, for tomorrow will care for itself. Each day has enough trouble of its own" (Matthew 6:33, 34).

Live one day at a time—God will take care of your future!

Friday: Why Is He Staring At Me?

Lord,
Every day I'm faced with situations
  that involve the opposite sex.
Sometimes they flatter me,
Sometimes they make my heart beat faster,
Sometimes they send me off
  into a world of daydreams.
Oh, Father, keep my imaginations pure.
Keep my eyes on You and my dreams
  in tune with Your will.
And send me the greatest human love
  that I can ever know,
If it's in Your plan for me.
Today, and always, I thank You for YOUR love
And I give it first place in my heart.

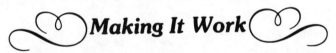

Making It Work

1. Write the biggest problem regarding men that you face as a woman.
    a. Try to analyze why there is a problem; list the reasons.
    b. See if you can think of ways to alleviate the problem with God's help.
2. Prayerfully consider whether or not your "romantic" side is committed to God. Ask Him to help you to continuously submit your emotions to Him.

6
Saturday
What Could Be Better Than Time Off?

Jennifer awoke at six o'clock sharp. She reached for the alarm, but miraculously, it wasn't ringing! Then all at once, with great delight, she realized that it was Saturday.

She pushed the white curtain aside and peeked out the window. The sky was pearly grey, and the wind stirred the trees and clouds, promising rain showers later in the day. She was still drowsy, so she pulled the comforter around her, smiled contentedly and snuggled back into bed. Two days off work! What would she do? First she'd get up in an hour or so, build a little fire in the fireplace and make herself a cup of coffee. Maybe she'd even grind some fresh coffee— since she had the time.

After she had eased into the morning, she would clean the house, water the plants and get all the "busy work" out of the way. By afternoon she would be finished and she would have time to begin reading her new book. She had been longing to bake some chocolate chip cookies to take to her grandmother, too. But most of all, she just hoped to relax. To slow down. To do just what she felt like doing with all those wonderful, leisure hours. What could be better than time off?

For most of us who work, life would be terrible without our blessed Saturdays. The anticipation usually begins on Friday afternoon, and by the time we arrive home we are looking forward to the days ahead with an almost breathless sense of excitement. There is nothing like a little freedom to put us back in touch with ourselves and with the "real" world we have to leave behind us when we go to work.

But leisure time doesn't really begin on Saturday morning. It begins every evening when you or I arrive home after work. Do we put those spare moments to good use so we'll have more time on Saturday? How can we best utilize all our free hours in order to rejuvenate ourselves, to enjoy our families and friends to the utmost, and to prepare ourselves for the next day's or next week's work? It is really not as easy as it sounds!

Strange as it may seem, making the most of free time really begins with a little organization. And believe me, when I talk about organization, I am not talking about something that comes naturally to me. But I have learned that without it, things just don't get done.

There are some things in life that just simply have to

be done, or our little worlds are likely to come crashing around us rather quickly. So, before we even begin to think about Saturday, let's take a look at week-in, week-out duties that all of us face.

First of all, we have to eat. Groceries have to be bought, food has to be prepared, meals have to be served (particularly if we have husbands and children) and dishes have to be done. Few of us can afford to eat out often, so we've got to expect some food-related responsibilities.

Second, things get out of place in our houses. We use the phone book and don't put it away. Glasses get left on the coffee table. Newspapers get spread around, clothes fail to be re-closeted. And, again, with families, the clutter compounds itself dramatically.

Third, clothes require washing, ironing and hanging up, as do sheets, towels and other odds and ends of laundry.

Fourth, dust accumulates, mirrors and windows virtually grow fingerprints, bathrooms need scouring and on and on and *on*.

Depressing, isn't it? Most definitely, unless you are one of those rare souls who thrives on housework. It can really get to be a hassle when you work eight hours, travel a half hour each way to and from work and then have to contend with housekeeping. So how, you ask, can organization help?

If you make some rules for yourself and keep them, you will know what to expect when you get home from work. If you *know* that on Tuesday night you're going to do a couple of loads of washing, you won't be nearly so depressed *Monday* night when you notice that the dirty laundry is building up.

Or suppose you have declared Thursday night as clean-the-bathroom night. You'll find that going in, cleaning it and getting it over with is a lot easier than sitting on the couch, procrastinating and dreading the task.

Try making yourself a mental schedule for the week. If you're *really* organized, you might even write it down! If you are at all like me, you'll probably rebel a little at the idea of a schedule, but there really is some security in knowing when things are *going* to be done. And there is certainly a wonderful relief in knowing that they *are* done and don't need to be thought about again for another whole week!

There are also some things that I try to do during the week, just to keep the house *looking* tidy, at least on the surface. Unless I'm outrageously late, I try to make the bed every morning. That way when I get home from work, the bedroom doesn't look like a hurricane went through. I also try my best to do the dishes every night—unless there are only two or three because we've eaten out. When I get up in the morning, the kitchen is neat and I have the feeling that things are at least somewhat under control.

We live in a fairly dusty area, and with dark wood furniture the living room can start looking pretty terrible by Tuesday, even if I cleaned on Saturday. A few months ago I solved this problem by buying a $1.98 feather duster. By using it once or twice during the week, I keep the furniture surfaces reasonably clean without having to move countless books, pictures, plants, or vases.

Perhaps as important as clean dishes, made beds or dusted surfaces is tidiness. A clean room that is cluttered *looks* worse than a room that's not so clean but uncluttered. If we attend to these things during the week, our houses won't get out of control before the weekend rolls around.

Besides things we *must* do, we all have things that we *like* to do in our spare time. Some of us enjoy painting, sewing, cooking, writing letters, sculpting. And whatever your favorite endeavor may be, it is important. Why? Because it allows you to fulfill the side of your personality that your job doesn't involve.

There are secretaries who are artists. There are teachers who are musicians. There are clerks and factory workers who are seamstresses and poets and gardeners. And for us to be really happy, I think it is important to polish every facet of our lives to its fullest sparkle. That way we become complete.

And—that way we *unwind.* Sometimes we arrive at home so tied in knots that we can't get our minds off our jobs for hours. We stew over something we said. Or we try to think up a new idea. Or we worry (yes, we all do it) about something that is about to happen. These mental processes accomplish very little, except to tire us.

What we really need to do is fill our extra hours with worthwhile, pleasant activities that make us feel like we are doing something valuable with our lives— activities which take our minds off the daily grind.

Saturday: What Could Be Better Than Time Off?

Do you have outside interests? Sometimes I marvel at women who can sew or knit or do needlepoint. I am sure that attempting such things in my spare time hours would frustrate me fifty times more than my job does! And yet, writing would probably depress someone else terribly. We have to fill our hours with things we enjoy, not simply with things we feel we must do.

I long ago decided that I would never again feel guilty that I wasn't a dedicated cook and baker, creating marvelous delicacies for my friends and family. I don't particularly like doing it, so I don't spend hours trying to develop an interest in it.

Of course, this doesn't mean that if you don't like keeping your house clean or doing dishes or laundry that you don't have to do these things. Some things, dreary as they seem, still remain necessary unless you can afford hired help!

Sometimes even the things we like doing best can be hard to stick with. Finishing projects is a lot harder than starting them! The example that is most obvious to me right now deals with this book. As I've said before, my everyday job is where the Lord has put me for now. But writing is what I really feel led to do with my life.

When I felt that this book was something the Lord was encouraging me to write, I had to say yes, even though I had a full-time job. That meant writing after work in the evenings, on weekends, on days off or whenever I could find the time.

It seemed simple enough in theory. But I have been

amazed at the number of distractions that have come along—TV shows, telephone calls, visits with friends, reading old books for the third time. Then, of course, Christmas is one remarkably long distraction. It goes on and on. It really takes discipline for me to keep writing, much as I enjoy it.

Working mothers have a very special dilemma: spending enough time with their kids after putting in an entire day's work elsewhere. It is especially difficult when children are small and need lots of love and attention.

The best advice I know—and it comes from those who actually face this situation—is to set aside a period of time each day that belongs to the children. This is a time when they know you will be there to listen, to play, to cuddle or to care.

Oh, but it's hard to have enough hours in a day to devote to everything and everyone important! Even a husband can be a problem. Even if *you* have worked all day, many husbands feel that *they* are the ones who need sympathy, attention and a listening ear. Rare is the spouse who feels that you and he must share the household responsibilities because you're sharing the wage earning.

I am certainly no marriage counselor, but this I do know from experience: Keeping frustrations, annoyances and anger bottled up inside accomplishes nothing. Discuss the circumstances with your spouse—preferably when you are calm and in your right mind! Tell him gently, lovingly, how you feel. Together, if possible, pray and ask God to show you what to do. Just don't expect your husband to read your mind. He may be wonderful in many other ways, but I'll bet he can't do that!

So, most of the housework is done, and it's Saturday morning. Why not make Saturday Husband Day or Family Day? What is your husband's favorite meal? What have you been promising your kids you would do with them? Have you taken the time to talk to your husband about *his* job, *his* problems, *his* world during the past busy week? Have you played "pretend" with your littlest one or had a heart-to-heart talk with your oldest?

Maybe you have always thought of Saturday as *your* day and you resent the idea of devoting your spare time to others. But let's think back to chapter one where we talked about the children's jingle that tells us how to spell JOY:

J-esus
O-thers
Y-ourself

Since Sunday is your day to spend with God, to worship Him in your heart and to refresh yourself spiritually, how about dedicating at least part of Saturday to others?

The single woman who doesn't have an immediate family to care for can give part of her day to others, too. Suppose you tell someone at the senior citizens' home that you will come in for a few hours Saturday to help the old folks write letters or read. Suppose you visit an invalid, or get a hospital list from the church and make rounds for an hour or two. Suppose you write to a great aunt in the midwest. Or send a little gift to a school teacher who helped you along the way.

Now this I say, he who sows sparingly shall also reap sparingly; and he who sows bountifully shall also reap bountifully. Let each one do just as he has purposed in his heart; not grudgingly or under compulsion; for God loves a cheerful giver.

And God is able to make all grace abound to you, that always having all sufficiency in everything, you may have an abundance for every good deed (II Corinthians 9:6-8).

This is something about which God has been speaking to me a great deal recently. When the Bible talks about giving, we usually think of money. And we *should* give money, for we are expected to give back to God a portion of what He has given us. But how about time? I have often said to myself that time is just as valuable as money. Yet how much of *my* spare time do I give back to God willingly?

By giving of ourselves to others we are, in effect, giving back to God some of the time that He has given to us. Jesus explains the concept in Matthew 25:

"But when the Son of Man comes in His glory, and all the angels with Him, then He will sit on His glorious throne. And all the nations will be gathered before Him; and He will separate them from one another, as the shepherd separates the sheep from the goats; and He will put the sheep on His right, and the goats on the left. Then the King will say to those on His right, 'Come, you who are blessed of My Father, inherit the kingdom prepared for you from the foundation of the world.

" 'For I was hungry, and you gave Me something to eat; I was thirsty, and you gave Me drink; I was a stranger, and you invited Me in; naked, and you clothed Me; I was sick, and you visited Me; I was in prison, and you came to Me.'

"Then the righteous will answer Him, saying, 'Lord, when did we see You hungry, and feed You, or thirsty, and give You drink? And when did we see You a stranger, and invite You in, or naked, and clothe You? And when did we see You sick, or in prison, and come to You?'

"And the King will answer and say to them, 'Truly I say to you, to the extent that you did it to one of these brothers of Mine, even the least of them, you did it to Me' " (Matthew 25:31-40).

Our time *and* our money belong to God. He wants us to give it freely back to Him. And when we do, He blesses us. What we sow, we reap!

We can also give some of our time back to God by being hospitable. Did you know that Christians are specifically instructed to open their homes to others? "Be hospitable to one another without complaint" (I Peter 4:9).

Maybe you are more gregarious than I, but inviting people over is not one of my favorite things. It seems like a lot of work, a lot of cleaning up. It is something that neither my husband nor I find to be a natural thing to do. And yet, once our friends have arrived and we are all sitting down talking and laughing and eating, I am *always* glad we did it. My husband and I have come to realize that constantly keeping to ourselves, staying home and not reaching out, can be a form of selfishness.

In all areas of our daily lives we need to strive for balance. While keeping to oneself continually may be a form of selfishness, constant activity may be an escape. If this is our pattern of living, we need to ask ourselves, *from what are we hiding?*

Some people are "workaholics." These individuals are doing something every minute of their lives. If they don't have their week-day job to do, they work hectically in the garden. If they aren't doing that, they are bustling off to visit a friend or to take part in some other kind of activity. This can be a wonderful personality trait that makes for productivity. But it can also mean that we don't want to be left alone to think for even a minute.

Strange as it may seem, people who sleep all day and people who work all day both have the same goal—

escape from reality.

There are times in our lives when sitting around in our nightgown until three in the afternoon is the greatest therapy in the world, and there are times when it's best to be busy, very productive with our spare-time hours. But time is short; we must find a balance between the two, and thereby come to know ourselves better.

In thinking about our use of time, I wrote this poem:

HOURGLASS

When faced with eternity
Man
Is unable to stand.
He cries out in fear
And seeks to escape.

When faced with a lifetime
Man
Is uncertain.
He grasps at the palpable
And ignores the invisible.

When faced with a year
Man
Is a dreamer.
He makes extensive plans
And accomplishes little.

When faced with an hour
Man
Is bored.
He watches his clock
And longs for the rapid passing of time.

When considering man,
God
Created hours to simplify eternity.
But man reversed the perspective,
And assumed that He had created eternity
From a vast accumulation of his wasted hours.

Planning the coming week just a little on Saturday will continue the smoothly organized schedule of the working woman. Is transportation arranged? Are meals planned for the coming week, including lunches if they are to be taken along? Are clothes clean? Ironed? Sometimes, if we have a pretty good idea of what we are going to wear each day of the week, it keeps us from being quite so late in the mornings, especially *Monday* morning!

Saturdays are great for plucking eyebrows, doing hair color, and painting nails and toes. And a long, leisurely bubble bath can be an absolutely heavenly experience.

All in all, Saturday is a wonderful day. It is a day for sleeping in just a little. It is a day for getting the house in order and for reorganizing chores. It is a day for doing the leisure time activities that we most enjoy. It is a Family Day, a Husband Day and an Others Day. It is a

Hospitality Day, and a day for planning the week to come.

And as with every other day of the week, Saturday is, indeed, a gift from God. It is a period of time that He has given us to use as we think best—serving Jesus, helping others and giving you and me a much needed rest.

Lord,
Thank You for today . . .
I was weary and You gave me rest.
I was hungry for a little free time and You provided it.
I was nearly ill from the pressures of my job, and
  You sent healing to my soul.
Help me to be like You, taking the time to
Feed the starving,
  clothe the naked,
    visit the sick.
For all time is Your possession,
And You have graciously loaned me a Saturday
Once a week.
Help me to give part of it back to You
And to fully savour the rest.
And, Lord,
Thanks for understanding my needs so well.

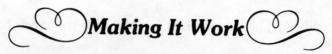

Making It Work

1. Make out a "schedule" for the week, allowing adequate time for chores, rest and recreation, as well as prayer and reading God's Word.
2. List people with whom you could "share" your Saturdays, and ways that you could help or cheer others in your spare time.

7
Sunday
It Was A Good Week,
Wasn't It?

The clock struck five as Anne sat at the table, reading, thinking and watching the day fade into shadows outside the window. It was Sunday afternoon, late in September. She had been to church that morning, and had spent a quiet day listening to some favorite albums, finally getting into a Christian book she had been saving for just such an occasion. It had been a good day, and despite the fact that the weekend was over, she felt good inside.

She had some difficult circumstances to face at work tomorrow, and she had been putting them aside for two days, trying not to dwell on them. But now she concentrated on them in light of the words to a hymn that the congregation had sung that morning, "strength for today and bright hope for tomorrow. . . blessings all mine and ten thousand beside."

She smiled a little. Why had she been dreading

tomorrow when she knew all along that God was in control? There was absolutely nothing to worry about! Not one thing could come into her life that God didn't allow to be there—work difficulties included. Tomorrow would be a good day, because she would have a chance to see just what God was going to do with her problem! Instead of apprehension, she felt a warm, peaceful feeling.

She gently closed the book, walked across the room to the couch, where she knelt to pray, "Thank You, Lord, for taking away my worry. Thank You for giving me 'bright hope for tomorrow.' And most of all, Lord, thank You for Sunday and the past days, too. It was a good week, wasn't it?"

I would be the first to admit that Sunday used to be a terrible day for me. Inevitably, I wanted to sleep late, and I resented having to get up and go to church. By the time I got there I would be cranky and critical. And after church was over, the rest of the day seemed like a countdown until Monday morning!

I can't say today that I have complete victory over this problem. But it has gotten better, and I think I know the reason: I have been trying to give Sundays to God. It sounds a little silly to say that, perhaps, since we call Sunday the "Lord's Day." But what I mean is this: Sunday used to be a day of obligation to me. Now it is a day of worship.

Since this way of looking at Sunday has helped me, I think it may help you, too. The first problem I faced was that of going to church. I must confess right here and now that going to church is not easy for me. I don't know why it is, but I dread it until I am actually there. Then I'm nearly always glad I have gone.

Sometimes it makes me feel better to look around the church and to realize that a lot of other people are going through some of the same things that I'm experiencing. They know Jesus, too, and I'm really not so all alone after all!

Do we have to go to church? God has instructed us to join together in worship with other Christians. He wants us to be taught in His Word and to share our Christian lives with others:

> Not forsaking our own assembling together, as is the habit of some, but encouraging one another; and all the more, as you see the day drawing near (Hebrews 10:25).

"Assembling together" takes place through Sunday morning and evening worship services, training hours, mid-week Bible studies and prayer times, and other gatherings of Christians—formal or informal—for the purpose of worship, instruction, encouragement and fellowship. Assembling together with other believers is one of God's ways of keeping us encouraged in the faith.

Of course there are countless excuses for not going to church—I've used most of them myself. You're too tired. The preacher's a bore. The choir sings off key. There are a lot of phonies there who aren't really Christians at all.

No matter what the excuses may be (and they may all be true!), God has told us to join together in worship—for our own good.

I am beginning to think that Satan has a special little game plan that he uses against me on Sundays. When I was a young girl, I have a very clear memory of Sunday morning squabbles in our house. Daddy would get irritated with Mother because she was taking too long to get ready, and he would go sit in the car with the engine idling for fifteen minutes, trying to hurry her along.

Meanwhile, she would become extremely annoyed with me because I wasn't getting my act together the way I was supposed to. We would eventually all end up in the car, but we would be so griped, defensive and generally fed up with each other that we were barely speaking by the time we arrived at church!

Until I got married, I thought this problem was peculiar to my immediate family. But at times the same thing has happened to my husband and me! We get angry with each other while we are trying to get to church on time. And the strange part about it is that it never happens when we are trying to get to *work* on time—just church. I always end up thinking, "I'd be better off not going to church at all than being this uptight!"

Does Satan ever do the same thing to you? Perhaps not. Maybe instead he tells you that you need rest after working all week. Or he convinces you that it's not worth the hassle of getting the kids ready. Or that you'd better not offend the people visiting you.

Sometimes, of course, there are legitimate reasons for not attending church. And I don't agree with those who categorically state that it is a sin not to go, no matter what your reason might be. But if you have grown lazy or you have listened to Satan's excuses and added a few of your own, take a closer look at your church attendance, just as I have to do occasionally.

While we are on the subject of church, let's talk a bit about serving God within the church structure. Sunday schools often need teachers. And piano players. And secretaries. Youth groups need sponsors and homes where they can get together for socializing. Choirs need singers. Has God been speaking to you about doing something for Him in relation to your church?

All of us aren't gifted teachers, but we can still make pretty good cookies for Vacation Bible School. We can't all play the piano, but most of us are capable of taking roll or passing out Sunday school papers.

Let's listen carefully to what God is saying. Let's volunteer our humblest talents and let the Lord increase them. And let's remember—Sunday school and youth groups, for some children, are the only contact with Christ that they have in their entire lives. It is up to us to help make that contact worthwhile.

We talked in the last chapter about giving part of our time to God. Sometimes that means "emptying our pockets" of spare time, and letting Him give time back to us. But let's remember, God loves a *cheerful* giver. If the time we give Him is given resentfully, we may as well forget giving it. He would rather we didn't. And

Sunday: It Was A Good Week, Wasn't It?

chances are, the folks at church would rather we didn't
too!

"But," you cry desperately, "I don't have time.
Remember? I have to *work* five days a week! Let the
housewives do the church work. I'm *busy*."

Did you know that a lot of housewives have less time
than we working women? Women with babies or
small children who haven't started school yet are on
their feet, active, from about 6 A.M. until the children's
bedtime. And then they are so exhausted they can do
little but sit and stare until they go to bed! Let's
never feel that homemakers and full-time mothers are
gifted with more free time than we, busy as *we* are.

I can't talk about church activities without bringing
up a problem that I have faced, and maybe you have,
too. Perhaps, for example, you joined the choir at your
church. You went to the first practice and found that
half the time was spent in talking about the people who
weren't there, and the conversation was not carried on
in the spirit of Christian love.

Or you went to a Sunday school teachers' meeting
and noticed that there was a great deal of bickering
and sniping between the teachers and the Sunday
school coordinator. You couldn't help thinking, "This
is just as bad as the way non-Christians act at work!"

Churches can, indeed, be plagued with ego
problems, spiritual pride, gossip, unkindness and a
myriad of other un-Christlike qualities. And the reason
is that churches are full of people—people like you and
me. And people—like you and me—are not perfect.
So what are we supposed to do?

Well, what we *aren't* supposed to do is judge! Just as we are not put in the position of judging non-believers, we are also expected to overlook the failings of fellow Christians. After all, we undoubtedly have a few faults ourselves!

We should always pray for our Christian brothers, especially when we see them stumbling. And we should pray humbly, asking God to keep us from falling into the same temptations.

And, as we are to do in the world, we should be lights to other Christians. Being a light to others often means simply being a good example. And always, *always* in a spirit of humility.

If you are a relatively new Christian, you may find some of these church-related problems discouraging. You may even find yourself doubting the effectiveness of your newfound faith, when you see more mature Christians acting in an un-Christlike manner.

This may seem to be a strange parallel to you, but it makes sense to me: The program that Weight Watchers has set up has changed the lives of countless people. In theory and in practice, the program works. Still, there are a lot of fat people walking around who went to Weight Watchers for help and still didn't lose weight. Does that mean Weight Watchers offers an ineffective means of losing weight? No! It means that *the people who didn't lose weight didn't follow the program correctly!*

The same thing holds true for Christians who don't act or live the way they should. The program works. The Bible says that when we are reborn we are completely changed.

> Therefore if any man is in Christ, he is a new
> creature; the old things passed away; behold,
> new things have come (II Corinthians 5:17).

If we are not as changed as we should be, the reason is simple: We haven't followed the Word of God closely enough; we haven't spent enough time with the Lord to be perfected.

Worshiping God in church is important and necessary to us as Christians, but worship doesn't stop when church is over. Worship continues when we look at a breathtaking mountain, snowcapped and glistening in the sun, when we realize that God made it, and when we thank Him for it. Worship continues when we sing a Christian song to the Lord as we are driving alone in the car. *Going* to church is an act of obedience. What we do, feel and think *during* church is worship. Worship is an outpouring of the heart.

> This is pure and undefiled religion in the sight
> of our God and Father, to visit orphans and
> widows in their distress, and to keep oneself
> unstained by the world (James 1:27).

Are you in touch with God through the reading of His Word and through prayer? This also is worship. It is definitely a matter of self-discipline in the beginning. It means *making* yourself sit down, read the Bible and pray. If you are not doing it, you probably don't miss it.

Once you get started, however, you will find that you really long for the time that you have with Him. It makes all but the things we do for Him seem very insignificant somehow, and puts everything else into proper perspective.

There are three ways we can really get to know God. One is through His Word, the Bible. It is a means that He has chosen to reveal Himself to us in our lifetime. Another way He reveals Himself to us is through answered prayer. A third way is through His Spirit, who lives within us all if we are reborn Christians. If we do not read the Word or pray, that cuts out two ways of knowing God better!

Plan to read your Bible in the way you would any other book, starting at the beginning and reading through it to get its message. Yet, unlike other books, you can begin with any section, or book of the Bible, and learn from it. Perhaps you can start out with the Gospels of Mark and John. After you've read and absorbed their content, go to the books of Ephesians and Philippians. At times a single verse or group of verses will speak to your need at the time. It takes real study of His Word to know God and His Son Jesus Christ better.

In addition to Bible reading, you will want to talk often to God in prayer. While you are praying, confess your sins and mistakes to Him every day. Ask for His forgiveness, through Christ. This will help you grow and develop as a Christian and you will see your life changing. Sometimes it is not too pleasant to admit the negative things we have said or done. But if we don't, we tend to forget them, pretending that we haven't done anything wrong. But the Bible says:

> If we say that we have no sin, we are deceiving ourselves, and the truth is not in us. If we confess our sins, He is faithful and righteous to forgive us our sins and to cleanse us from all unrighteousness (I John 1:8, 9).

The Bible is a *living* Word. As we change, it speaks to us in different ways. And since it is the way God has chosen to reveal Himself to us, we must continuously seek to know it more fully. No one, not even the greatest Bible scholar the world has known, has ever reached a total knowledge of God's Word. Even if we did have total knowledge, we would need continuous reminding to keep us on the right path.

Does prayer really work? I confess that I don't know just *how* it works, or *why* God wants to hear requests from us when He has said that He already knows what we need before we ask. But prayer does indeed work. Remarkable things happen every day when we are in constant prayer.

Prayer doesn't stop when we are through with our devotions. It is a continuous "attitude" that we should maintain. This attitude says, "God is with me every moment of my life; He knows what is happening; He is guarding and directing me every step of the way—so I should be talking to Him!"

Prayer doesn't mean just asking for things; it means thanking Him for beauty; it means sharing a joke with Him; it means telling Him that we love Him. And besides *wanting* to do all that, we are *instructed* in God's Word to pray: "Rejoice always; pray without ceasing" (I Thessalonians 5:16,17).

Spending time in the Word and in prayer is the way we are to put on the "armor" of God:

> Therefore, take up the full armor of God, that you may be able to resist in the evil day, and having done everything, to stand firm. Stand firm therefore, having girded your loins with truth, and having put on the breastplate of righteousness, and having shod your feet with the preparation of the gospel of peace; in addition to all, taking up the shield of faith with which you will be able to extinguish all the flaming missiles of the evil one. And take the helmet of salvation, and the sword of the Spirit, which is the word of God (Ephesians 6:13-17).

It may seem out of date for us to think about "armor" and "warfare," but the fact that Satan attacks us isn't out of date at all. And if we are not prepared, we will sin and stumble off the right track. It is God's Word and prayer that keep us spiritually fit and healthy, just as good food and sleep keep us physically well.

Let's take a look at the armor that God is talking about in this part of His Word. I am certainly not a great Bible expositor, but maybe together we can find out what God means when He talks about each part of His warrior's protection.

"Gird your loins with truth." What does TRUTH mean? Truth means honesty—honesty with ourselves and honesty with others. Are we honest people in all areas of our lives? In our dealings with people on a business level? In our personal lives? Are our motives sound? Have we learned to fib to get around difficult circumstances? We need to learn the value of real honesty and to make honesty part of our lives every day.

"Breastplate of righteousness." The dictionary defines righteous as "acting in accord with moral or divine law: free from guilt or sin." We can wear our RIGHTEOUSNESS in two ways: First, by living our lives with a healthy, moral attitude we can conduct ourselves "in accord with moral or divine law." This means wanting to do the right thing and making every effort to keep our minds free of evil and unhealthy thoughts.

Second, as Christians we can live our lives free from guilt or sin in God's eyes, because He has forgiven us and justified us. Justified means "just-as-if-I-hadn't sinned." As far as our position with God is concerned, we are guiltless and sin-free.

When we feel guilt for something we have done, we need only go to God, confess our sin to Him and then go on as if it hadn't happened. We thus "wear" righteousness—by making an effort to live God's way and by knowing that we are perfect in God's sight.

"Shod your feet with the preparation of the gospel of peace." There are two kinds of PEACE. There is peace with God, which we have because we have put

our faith in Jesus. Jesus *is* our peace with God. And there is peace with men—possible through the work of God's Spirit within our lives. When we are at peace with men we are not irritable, quarrelsome, jealous or super-opinionated. We will, instead, display the attributes of Christ toward all people. And we will try to put love first in our lives.

"Helmet of salvation." Do we *know* inside that we are saved? Not only are we safe from eternal punishment, but in Jesus we are safe from harm. Nothing can come into our lives that God does not allow for our good or for the good of His work in the world. And because of this, we can also have salvation from fear.

"The sword of the Spirit which is the Word of God." Are we continuously aware of God's Word? This is easily accomplished by reading our Bible, memorizing passages that are important to us and retaining the essence of what the Word teaches. David said, "Thy word have I hid in mine heart, that I might not sin against thee" (Psalm 119:11, KJV).

"In addition to all, taking up the shield of faith." It is wonderful to know that God is in control at all times. That knowledge, very simply, is the FAITH we need to quench the enemy's "burning missiles." Our lives belong to God; He is taking care of us. We have nothing to worry about!

Let's live our lives by being prepared the way God wants us to be prepared. Let's be continually aware of truth, humbly cognizant of our righteousness in Christ. Let's maintain an unwavering attitude of peace. Let's be aware and thankful for our salvation—unafraid because of Christ. Let's continue to acquaint ourselves with scripture, and always be conscious that God is in control of our daily lives.

Not by accident, the verse that follows Paul's discussion of armor is this:

> With all prayer and petition pray at all times in the Spirit, and with this in view, be on the alert with all perseverance and petition for all the saints (Ephesians 6:18).

Besides wearing the armor of God, we are instructed, almost in the same breath, to be in prayer, communicating with God about everything. We are to be alert, watching for answers. We are to be persistent, not giving up on "hard" cases. And we are to be in prayer for other Christians because they have to face the "enemy," too.

Sunday, for us, is a day of preparation. It is the day that God has given us to get ready for the week ahead. He has told us *how* to get ready: by worshiping, by putting on the "armor" that He has provided, by praying for others.

If we spend our Sundays using the wonderful gifts that God has given us, we will be able to begin a new week rested mentally, filled with God's Spirit, confident in His control over our lives.

So, as the sun sets on Sunday, another week has all but begun. Fast as the weekend flew, it is time to go back to work tomorrow morning. Are we ready?

Do we know *why* we have the jobs that we have? Yes. Because God has put us where we are so that we can shine as lights for Him in the world.

Do we like ourselves well enough to shine as lights? Yes. Because He loves us, He is making us valuable and beautiful people by His love.

Is it possible for us to get along with others as we work? Yes. Because the Spirit that lives within us is the Spirit of God's love which makes us able to love even the most unlovable people.

Can we socialize with non-Christians without weakening our spiritual lives and without jeopardizing the example that we are setting? Yes. Because our purpose is not simply to have a good time, but to be Christian lights wherever we go. With His Word in our hearts we can avoid the sins that tempt us and be a good example for Him.

Can our romantic selves be fulfilled and still be committed to God? Yes. Of all those who love us, God loves us most. He knows who and what is best for us, and if we truly trust Him, He will give us the happiest, most love-filled lives we could ever desire.

Tomorrow is Monday again. But let's look forward to it a little more than usual. Monday is the beginning of an adventure—an adventure of answered prayer, of newly-revealed truth, of standing apart from the crowd, knowing that we are special. Monday is the beginning of another week in the service of the King— and not just any king, but our Father the King of Kings who has given us the world to conquer with His love.

Sunday: It Was A Good Week, Wasn't It?

We have a lot to do—and there are Just Five Days Till Friday!

Father,
Take my Sunday and bless it for me.
Teach me to worship You,
Teach me to use my gifts in Your church.
Teach me to prepare myself for the week ahead
with the armor that You have provided.
And let my life be one of continuous worship,
Monday through Sunday,
Morning through Evening.
Let my days and hours be an offering of love to You.
For because You love me, Lord,
I love You.

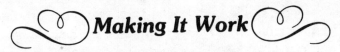 ## Making It Work

1. Evaluate your feelings about attending church.
   a. Are you "forsaking the assembly"?
   b. Do you like church? If so, good. If not, try to list reasons why. Ask God to help you see and to resolve whatever church-related difficulties you may have.
2. Write some ways that you could serve God within His church. Then volunteer.
3. Make a list of people who need your prayer. Pray for them every day after you've read your Bible.